Changing Security Agendas and the Third World

Changing Security Agendas and the Third World

LLOYD PETTIFORD
and
MELISSA CURLEY

With an afterword by Stephen Chan

PINTER
London and New York

PINTER
A Cassell imprint
Wellington House, 125 Strand, London WC2R 0BB
370 Lexington Avenue, New York, NY 10017-6550

First published 1999
© Lloyd Pettiford, Melissa Curley and Stephen Chan 1999

Apart from any fair dealing for the purposes of research or private study or criticism or review, as permitted under the Copyright, Designs and Patents Act 1988, this publication may not be reproduced, stored or transmitted, in any form or by any means or process, without the prior permission in writing of the copyright holders or their agents. Except for reproduction in accordance with the terms of licences issued by the Copyright Licensing Agency, photocopying of whole or part of this publication without the prior written permission of the copyright holders or their agents in single or multiple copies whether for gain or not is illegal and expressly forbidden. Please direct all enquiries concerning copyright to the publishers.

British Library Cataloguing-in-Publication Data
A catalogue for this book is available from the British Library.

ISBN 1-85567-538-2

Library of Congress Cataloging-in-Publication Data
Pettiford, Lloyd, 1966–
    Changing security agendas and the Third World/Lloyd Pettiford and Melissa Curley; with an afterword by Stephen Chan.
      p. cm.
    Includes bibliographical references and index.
    ISBN 1-85567-538-2 (hardcover)
    1. Security, International. 2. Sustainable development.
3. Developing countries—Foreign relations. I. Curley, Melissa, 1971– . II. Title.
JZ5588.P48 1999
327. 1′7′01–dc21   98-30980
                                                                                           CIP

Typeset by BookEns Ltd., Royston, Herts.
Printed and bound in Great Britain by Cromwell Press Limited, Trowbridge, Wiltshire

Contents

	Acknowledgements	vii
	Introduction: Contemporary Insights on Security	1
1.	Rethinking the Third World	21
2.	Opening the Can of Worms: Realism to Neorealism	41
3.	Critical Theory and Postmodernism: The Challenges	57
4.	Environmental/Ecological Philosophies and Security	73
5.	Engaging with Other Fields and Disciplines	93
6.	Security and Development: Exploring Conceptual and Practical Linkages	108
7.	Security and Sustainable Development	131
	Conclusions: The Future of Security?	147
	Afterword: Signing the Swamplands *Stephen Chan*	156
	Index	159

Acknowledgements

Since the proposal for this book was rather loosely based on my PhD thesis (University of Southampton, 1994), thanks should first go to Peter Calvert, my supervisor, and to all those people at Southampton and elsewhere who were recognized in my PhD acknowledgements. Thanks to Nana Poku for being involved with this book at the proposal stage; congratulations on your new family and we are sorry you were unable to contribute to the book. Thanks are also due to all those people at Nottingham Trent University who have helped us both, notably Stephen Chan for writing an afterword and reading drafts and Chris Farrands for reading drafts. Thank you also to all those people who contributed to our research in Bolivia, Laos, Vietnam, the United Kingdom, the United States and Australia, particularly Eivind Hovden, Jill Steans, Chris May, Parvarti Raghuram and Richard Johnson; there are many more, but they are too numerous to mention. Our friends and families have been crucial to the project and we would like to thank them too. Finally, thanks to those at Pinter for their helpful suggestions and encouragement from start to finish.

I would like to offer my personal thanks to several people, especially Melissa Curley for helping to finish a project that could not have been completed otherwise. Thanks to Peter Wilkin for helping me not to take academic matters too seriously; others have demonstrated to me the dangers of doing so. Thank you especially to Norksy. She has helped me not to take anything too seriously and at the same time given me things which are worthy of seriousness. If I have missed anyone out I am sorry and hope you will accept my honest faults as she does.

Lloyd Pettiford
October 1998

To Matthew Le Tissier

Introduction: Contemporary Insights on Security

About This Book

The aim of this book is to discuss and explain the International Relations (IR) security debate in both theoretical and practical terms. In relating this debate to the third world (and shifting conceptions of such a concept), in a manner which is relevant to students of IR theory, Development Studies (DS) and, to a lesser extent, environmental politics, we want to set up the debate for further consideration. What we are aiming to do is to provide the background for thinking about security (that is, pulling together contemporary debates) in such a way that our own thinking about this may be contextualized (Chapters 6 and 7); in this sense, we are hoping to provide a useful starting-point for students wanting to think about security (a solid grounding in the security debate) but we are also trying to go beyond this to say *something* to the debate itself, primarily about possible linkages with aspects of development.

During the late 1980s and early 1990s it was common to hear the opinion that 'the present period in world politics provides a particularly apposite historical conjuncture in which to re-examine the fundamentals, and even the meaning, of security' (Lawler, 1990, p. 125). After many years of doing so, we would argue that particularly apposite is a book which addresses this whole debate, which explains some of the positions being debated and which suggests that certain profitable avenues of possible research have, thus far, been neglected.

We should stress from the outset, however, that our aim is not to attach a single new *meaning* to security but to investigate new ways of attempting to understand the idea, as well as why and how these might be useful to students of a variety of disciplines. To clarify this point, we are looking to suggest that there are various *tools* which may be used in debates surrounding security. What we do not suggest is *a* definition of what security must be, nor of what exactly *common, comprehensive* or *environmental* security might involve in any detail. This does not mean that we regard these ideas as irrelevant or that we do not have our own biases on this subject; this is far from being the case, and our analysis will suggest preferences for looking at security in certain ways. However, we are seeking fundamentally to provide a book which looks at how and why security might be rethought in the context of a whole range of influences. In other words we are trying to suggest how readers might arrive at their own meaning.

The structure employed is quite simple; in this introduction we seek to sketch a short outline of the history of the security debate and, in a clear and simple fashion, to bring it up to date. The subsequent chapters look at what we mean by the 'third world' (and some of the problems and debates surrounding the concept) before explicitly exploring the theoretical side of security, critically engaging with, and/or suggesting linkages to, the thought and literatures of realism, neorealism, postmodernism, critical theory, environmentalism, ecologism, peace research, political geography and so on. Incorporated into each chapter will be an analysis of how different IR theorists have coped with the third world in their work, or not as the case may be, and how different theories have different importance in this context.

Chapter 1 on the third world is considered particularly important; we suggest that one cannot just look at security as if it were changing its position relative to a constant third world. One reason is that this almost implies an analytical emergence of problems which already existed, as if 'security' were just catching up with a solid third world 'reality'. We would argue that this is not *all* that is happening with 'security' or the 'third world'. Fundamentally, the idea of the third world is also changing in the manner in which it is understood/visualized and is being challenged so that *both* key ideas behind the book (security and third world) are actually being reconsidered or *moving around* in the social sciences. The end of the Cold War, the success of newly industrializing countries (NICs), the wealth of the Gulf States, the poverty of sub-Saharan Africa, as well as what might be termed the *peripheralization of the core*, all give us grounds for at least tentativeness regarding how we might now conceptualize and analyse the third world.

Chapters 1 to 5 are foundational, suggesting ways of thinking about shifting concepts. We then move to some concluding chapters; these are *our* conclusions, combining recent work on, for example, the linkages of IR/DS, the place of sustainable development within the security debate, redefining the third world (Poku and Pettiford, 1998), and redefining security, together with work on eco-philosophy to suggest new approaches, not only to security but also to its relationship to the third world. Our influences in terms of ideas of emancipatory security and the development literature on empowerment will be apparent. Though we introduce our work by summarizing that of others, we want at this stage to emphasize that this does not imply that we regard what we have written as an intellectual end-point. Rather, Chapters 6 and 7 present the current *position* of our own thinking; we hope they *contribute* to some new and alternative understandings of security, but they do not represent some logical culmination of thought on the subject!

Our conclusions make various suggestions as to how the IR security debate has influenced the discipline, where the debate is going, to what extent security remains a central organizing concept for IR scholars and, consequently, how it is likely to shape the discipline's future. Ultimately, we justify the dual-track approach of the book. As the security debate moves away from the state-centric problem-solving of the traditional definition, towards approaches which seek to stress the emancipatory potential of the idea, that debate now has much more relevance for those who are disempowered, especially in the face of today's global(ized) political economy (see, for example, Saurin, 1996a and 1996b). Our first task then is to contextualize our arguments further by looking at contemporary developments in the security debate, which we do by beginning with a brief and simple history.

Security and International Relations: A Brief and Simple History

Thinking About the Idea of Security

In everyday life, *relative* peace of mind may be possible but actual security, objectively or psychologically, is virtually impossible to attain: 'there is such an abundance of risk that it is impossible to objectively know all that threatens us' (Campbell, 1992). And, as Ulrich Beck convincingly argues, 'in advanced modernity the social production of wealth is systematically accompanied by the social production of risks' (1992, p. 19). Furthermore, for each one of us, security may be different (physical, economic, psychological) and is liable to change along with spatio-temporal context. The meaning of security is thus fluid.

Within the study of IR, however, security has historically had a fairly fixed meaning. Even so, it has still proved elusive, ironically enough, as will be seen, because the associated assumptions about how to attain it have contained the certainty of insecurity within them. This fixed meaning has lost its moorings in recent years and 'security' has become an essentially contested concept and an area of concern in IR rather than a precisely defined condition (see Krause and Williams, 1997). That this should only recently have happened might be considered surprising. This is especially so since power has long been a highly contested concept within the social sciences more generally. However, this has historical reasons which will be explained and which have led to the labelling of IR as the 'backward discipline' (George, 1994).

The debate over security has become extraordinarily complex, or at least contentious, in a short space of time. One side effect is that its multiple meanings often mingle imperceptibly in the literature and in discussion, without explicit recognition of this fact; this of course is a basic rationale behind our own project. For some this is destroying the intellectual coherence of 'security', making it more difficult to devise solutions to the 'real' problems, (for example, Walt, 1991) whilst for others, including this book's authors, it is offering some ideas of genuine relevance to more than an elite minority in world politics. We do, however, recognize the confusion which can be caused by picking over the differences between what might be different about human, true or comprehensive security. Accordingly, we try less to give definitions to particular terms (for example, environmental security) and more to outline why particular ways of thinking, emerging from certain literatures, might help us as we think about the notion of security.

It is particularly since the 1983 publication of the first edition of Buzan's highly influential book, *People, States and Fear,* that the concept has found itself redefined, reconceptualized, reshaped, re-theorized, re-examined, refigured, re-visioned and many more (see Tickner, 1995). The resulting conceptual muddle has allowed some to claim not so much a re-definition as a de-definition (Deudney, 1990 and 1991). The fundamental causes of this state of flux go beyond the notion of security, to encompass wider, especially epistemological and ethical, debates within the discipline, but it is basically an expression of dissatisfaction with a concept which had previously served well, contributing in no small measure, it has been argued, to the 'long nuclear peace' of the

Cold War world (see Williams, 1992). However, and though such work has its unsung pioneers (see Falk, 1978), with the end of the Cold War many working in IR theory started to question both the universal applicability and the validity of the concept. To understand why, we must first trace the origins and use of security in IR.

Security in International Relations

Traditionally, security in IR has been analysed from a Western historical perspective. *Both* sides of the realist–idealist debate, which dominated the early IR of the inter-war period, were preoccupied with the concerns of a *particular* type of *state*. This was entirely understandable in the sense that the debate was the product of a particular intellectual tradition, faithfully reflecting a particular process of historical and political development which could be traced at least to the Peace of Westphalia (Ayoob, 1986, p. 6; see also Ayoob, 1995). Whilst presented as polar opposites (with differences in how to achieve security), both realism and idealism are essentially conservative status-quo-orientated doctrines, concentrating on war avoidance (abolition or control) and with little room for concerns *within* the state, such as poverty and injustice, and inequalities in the social domain.

The failures of idealism were revealed most starkly by the Second World War. The idea that aggressors could be deterred by the collective action of the international community (collective security) was discredited and IR became dominated by realism, a theory whose basic premises posit a notion of sovereign states acting in a decentralized anarchic system, where conflict is endemic and security is managed by power-seeking and self-help. Most commonly described using the billiard ball analogy, economic considerations are subordinate to security considerations, and relative advantage is more important than absolute advantage. Perpetual peace is impossible; at best there can be stability through the adroit management of alliances that counterbalance potential hegemons. Thus realist security focuses on war, the ability to fight wars and the external threats to the state which might give rise to them (Wolfers, 1962).

Conceptual development of security was limited for a long time by the constricted parameters of this realist tradition. In the nuclear age, the IR sub-field of Strategic Studies dominated investigation of security, with the extremely tense nature of superpower rivalry such that it was felt absolutely vital to keep abreast of technical developments in weaponry, warning systems and so on. As Stanley Koffman (1977) persuasively argued, the connection between the powerful research institutions and foreign policy community in the United States in the 1970s and 1980s ensured that funding and institutional credibility was accorded to the academic study of 'security' within a defence framework. Within such a context, development of security (as a concept) was considered unnecessary and dangerous, in that to change notions of security would tamper with the delicate 'balance of terror' which had almost paradoxically ensured a peace of sorts after the Second World War.

The related field of Peace Studies/Research, and notions of structural violence, developed by Johan Galtung (amongst others) failed to seriously divert strategists from their primary task and fundamental beliefs about what did, or should, constitute security. Indeed, it could be argued that security in this intellectual form worked entirely *within* the realist paradigm, which was incommensurate with other intellectual ideas about conflict and co-operation such as those developed in Peace Studies. Even in the security debate today there has been little serious engagement between the Strategic Studies community and those involved in what could be termed critical security studies.

Hence the problematization of national security matters, outside the context of the developed states, was rarely considered, if at all, within the context of realism. Walter Lippman (1942) had argued that a nation can be considered secure if it does not have to sacrifice its core values (in order to avoid war) and is able, in the event of war, to maintain those values by victory in such a war. To make this notion of core values applicable to the third world it had to be reduced to a largely meaningless and minimalist definition of a nation's core values as (formal) political independence and territorial integrity (Maniruzzaman, 1982). The reality of many third world states as legally recognized actors by the international community but not as *social facts* meant that security fell significantly short of explaining or outlining what security might signify for such countries, where internal dimensions have been more important (see Thomas and Saravanamuttu, 1987). Therefore the third world and its specific structural location in the international system, both economically and politically, were unquestioned in the realist discourse of security. In other words there were particular ways in which the third world did not fit into the realist paradigm and thus its deviations in practical terms were not considered important or relevant in theoretical terms.

However, within Strategic Studies the third world *did* eventually become a consideration in the context of its militarization. It was argued that 'the growing military weight, economic power, and political influence of developing states require a re-examination of prevailing assumptions about their role and impact on regional and global security' (Kolodzeij and Harkavy, 1982, p. 363). The implication has often been that third world states would be less responsible than those in charge of the 'balance of terror' for many decades, since they have more to gain and less to lose (see Weiss and Kessler, 1991). Many third world leaders or peoples were thus demonized and branded as 'madmen', a trend which has only increased in the 1990s as evil 'others' were sought to replace the Soviet 'evil empire' of Reagan-speak. Of course wider critical questions of the West's role in encouraging third world militarization were, and are, of little relevance to the hard-nosed realists of Strategic Studies, concerned to manage the world as it 'is', never questioning how it got this way, or their own role in shaping it.

The incorporation of the third world into security studies was clearly inadequate from the point of view of third world states, and more especially the people, themselves. When seen as the maintenance of minimum values, 'security' has been used to justify keeping internal order at any cost, leading to repression and patterns of expenditure which have served extremely narrow sectional interests (see Chomsky, 1987 and Dunkerley, 1988). Thus survival of a particular regime became the essence of third world security and such an arrangement proved useful both to the superpowers and to third world governments themselves. If the national security interests of the regime in power are dressed up in the language of anti-communist rhetoric to lend it an air of legitimacy internationally, in reality it is only possible to recognize the security of a *particular* regime (Thomas and Saravanamuttu, 1987).

Throughout the world, many militaries (the focus of a traditional approach to security) have been primarily concerned with countering threats of internal subversion, whether externally sponsored or not – other threats have not been of prime concern. The often paranoiac countering of internal subversion has been detrimental to the quality of life of large numbers of people, not just directly but through spending on instruments of repression rather than on health and education, for instance. Furthermore, in adopting such an approach, security policies based on an acceptance of the realist approach to IR fail to identify the most pressing concerns of many people, especially in the world's poorer states for whom the real security dilemma is clearly how to survive until tomorrow (see Booth, 1990).

However, it has undoubtedly been the case that interaction among sovereign states on the one hand and greater identification of individuals with their respective states on the other *has* seen the security of individuals totally subsumed within the category of state security at the level of political analysis. Indeed, 'the citizen is expected to serve the state and look to it for security within the world order' (Calvert, 1988, pp. 9–10). Thus, while there has been much debate about the compatible or incompatible nature of state security with the security of the international system, and on the measures that could be taken to reconcile the two demands for security, the security of units below the level of the state has rarely, if ever, been an important point at issue in most Western IR discussions and analyses of the concept of security.

Changing Security and International Relations

Realism, whose view of security went unchallenged for such a long time, has provided a research area both as a positive guide and as a foil against which to test alternative theoretical paradigms. Today it is pitted against a multiplicity of theoretical challenges within IR, introducing challenges for the study of security. One of the simplest and earliest ways to look at these challenges was in terms of Banks' useful categorization of IR theory put forward in 1985 (Banks, 1985). According to Banks, whose categorization is not without problems, IR is a triangular inter-paradigm debate between realist, pluralist and structuralist approaches. Even using this simple categorization, we can begin to see some of the *kinds* of pressures and influences to which realist security has been susceptible, and some new potentialities for thinking differently about security.

A pluralist world-view sees science, technology and economics producing interdependence, forcing states to abandon some of their sovereignty and independence. This model assumes a tightly interdependent 'cobweb' world containing a multiplicity of sub- and supranational actors (for example, MNCs, IGOs, NGOs, NSMs and GROs) as well as the traditional nation-state. In such a setting, security considerations are said to be less about the principle of self-help and more about the idea of well-being; the international environment becomes more stable, and the likelihood of war decreases. Functional integration and international regimes facilitate further growth of interdependence providing an additional avenue for inter-state co-operation. Absolute, rather than relative, gains become the norm (Keohane, 1989) and security is not something which has to be sought by the isolated, individual state.

Meanwhile, structuralist insights into IR,[1] often Marxist-derived, see the discipline's dominant actors as classes, and emphasize the links of politics and economics. In contrast to the 'billiard ball' and 'cobweb' analogies (of realism and interdependence), the structuralist model has been likened to a 'multi-headed octopus'. Though the analogy is rather less useful as a heuristic device, the suggestion is that the octopus heads are connected to their surroundings by tentacles constantly sucking wealth from poor, weak peripheral areas of the global economy to rich, strong central ones. Structuralist insights emphasize the gross inequality in international relations and the structures which help to keep this inequality in place. Life in the periphery, for all but the minority, can easily be seen here as a constant struggle for survival or security.

The characterization of IR as an inter-paradigm debate is in many ways unsatisfactory and being used less and less; some of the problems will be implicitly revealed throughout this book, which, rather than exploring this debate, engages with the challenges presented by critical theory, postmodernism and the increasing influence of other disciplinary currents such as sociological ones. In some ways the security debate in IR has occurred *across* the inter-paradigm debate. (Often different IR paradigms use an undifferentiated notion of security to refer to different practices, values, processes and material states without considering epistemological or practical linkages between them.) In any case, Steve Smith characterizes the approach taken by Banks, and subsequently used by many others, as 'tenable' and as 'excellent for introducing' (1995, p. 19) and, whilst we are aware of its limitations, even as a pedagogic tool, it serves well the aims of an introductory chapter such as this; if we combine varying inter-paradigm debate assumptions regarding actors, interests, processes and outcomes in IR with Buzan's urging to be clear about referent objects of security, we can immediately see that pluralist and structuralist positions offer ontological challenges to realism which raise doubts about the prominent position of traditional definitions of security within the study of IR. Let us be clear about our caveat here: IR has come a long way since Buzan (1983) and Banks (1985), but they represent significant steps in allowing questions about security and the discipline more generally to come to the fore.

Simply thinking about the inter-paradigm debate in this way we can begin to see where some of the problems associated with the complexity of the security debate have emerged from. Debates about security have, in effect, taken place *across* the so-called paradigms. Consequently, an idea such as *environmental security* could be understood by a realist as pertaining to matters such as topography, access to resources or the use of the environment as a weapon; by a pluralist in terms of the role of NGOs, scientific epistemic communities (Haas, 1989) and the success of international environmental regimes; and by a structuralist in terms of the close linkages between Northern over-consumption, Southern poverty *and* environmental degradation. This example illustrates how levels of analysis, referent objects and significant and/or desired processes possible in environmental security compete. One aim of this book is to help readers identify and understand how security is used in different contexts across the paradigms and beyond, and crucially the significance of these differences for the third world.

In the particular context of this book and its third world focus we can see that in many countries well-being is denied the majority at the substate level, and security could reasonably be extended to the whole range of issues which do not constitute problems in the developed world. Many third world countries and their citizens are burdened by debt, environmental problems, ineffective administrative structures, ethnic divisions and weak economies. It must reasonably be asked, which is why we do, if security can, and should, be understood in the same way for such states as it is for those of the developed world (Booth, 1990).

Security has therefore come under closer scrutiny. From the early 1980s, Buzan noted that 'in its prevailing usage the concept is so weakly developed as to be inadequate' (1991, p. 1). Dissatisfaction with this state of affairs has seen an increasing body of literature develop on the subject, mainly suggesting a development of the concept in two respects. Realist definitions of security could be described, in two senses, as one-dimensional: that is, they concentrate on only one type of actor (the state) and on only one form of power (military) (see also Lukes, 1974). Newer definitions have sought to expand the range of actors deemed worthy of study on the one hand (vertical expansion) and the range of issues on the other (horizontal expansion). This has inevitably required quite different assessments of another essentially contested concept, that of power.

However, it is quite clear that some work on security has been more subtle and complex than other work. Our aim in this introduction is simply to sketch how security has moved from a solid, almost unchanging and unchallenged basis for analysis to an essentially contested concept, and to locate the beginnings of this change not simply in the end of the Cold War but in earlier debates within IR itself. So far then we have outlined where security has come from and why it has changed direction; before beginning a more detailed analysis of what security might become, how we want to rethink it and how this can be related to third world experience, we give more detail below in terms of the signposts IR has been following as well as some of the potential avenues for further consideration.

Security Today: Signposts and Directions

Whilst the challenges now facing most nations are not as immediately catastrophic as those confronted by the adversaries in the Cold War, actors at *all* levels of analysis face problems which may be disastrous and whose resolution may require international co-operation on an unprecedented scale. Accordingly, there has been a tendency to recognize the inadequacy of the previous definition of security by attempting to revise, rather than discard, it. In effect, security has developed out of necessity simply because there is a lot of insecurity in the world! However, it must surely be questioned whether the effort of squeezing complicated ideas, such as 'the individual' and 'ecology' (which have little to do with Morgenthau-like ideas of national interest defined as power), into a simply understood, predominantly realist concept is a worthwhile exercise (see Morgenthau, 1978; Deudney, 1991).

Considerable complications have arisen from the attempts to stretch security both vertically and horizontally, as described above, by incorporating more levels of analysis and more issues. By specifying referent objects other than the state, and considering more than the notion of military power, security can easily encompass an enormous range of actors and issues. It is possible to argue that the *securities* of many actors are intimately linked and that it is not profitable to study any given type of actor in isolation (atomistically) but rather as a part of a whole (holistically). However, in doing so, it is possible to regard all threats to human well-being as threats to security; confusion is highly likely, and everything 'bad' becomes a 'security concern' (see, for example, Deudney, 1990; Walt, 1991).[2] Those who attempt to overcome this problem, by seeking to limit the broadening of security in order to maintain its clarity, must justify the limits they impose in dealing with a particular scope and type of threat.

Barry Buzan has noted the dangers of conceit inherent in assuming that the present is in some way crucial. It may be that we would simply *like* to think we are living at the cutting edge of profound historical change. Such a tendency is only likely to be increased by the millennium. Whilst noting these dangers, Buzan (1995) goes on to conclude that we are indeed at the end of an era and entering a new one. Given this period of momentous historical change through which the world seems to be passing, a reappraisal of security, particularly a re-examination of the focus on military matters, seems entirely justified, whatever problems of clarity ensue. However, the problems caused by the rapidity of change mean new and finished theories have always been unlikely. Work currently being done is best seen as part of a process, united in the sense of a common feeling that the continued dominance of the previous simple definition could present a substantial barrier to progress in the understanding of international relations, though divided, fundamentally, over methodological, ontological and epistemological issues.[3] Thus the signpost leading us from a dissatisfaction with the traditional approach may be obvious, but the next steps are less certain and require the reflection that we urge throughout this book.

Of course arguing that traditional definitions of security are not as relevant as they once were does not deny that there were good reasons why a Strategic Studies approach came to have such weight in IR. It was *plausibly* argued by proponents of the approach that the danger of nuclear war was so great that its avoidance had to take priority over other issues. In stepping away from realist security we still believe that avoiding nuclear war is important! However, whilst the ending of the Cold War has not made the threat of nuclear war disappear, it has allowed other actors and issues to gain space within the security debate. This provides the fundamental point of departure for this book – to ask how this intellectual space has been created and how it helps us understand the development problems of the third world.

Before moving on to look in detail at the theoretical development of security and its relation to the third world, it is worth outlining some of the more significant contributions to the debate in order to give the flavour of what follows – in effect specific references to the processes described above. We take a look at the work of Buzan and Booth as well as making reference to processes of globalization and debates over global security which are gaining increasing currency. Our choice is neither random nor comprehensive but seeks to highlight various points which will be picked up throughout the book, especially in Chapters 2 to 5.

Barry Buzan has reached such a level of fame within the security debate that while not everyone likes what he has said on the subject, almost everybody, including the authors of this book, feels it necessary to make reference to him! Despite much relevant and interesting work by students of Peace Studies or environmentalists (see, for example, the work of Falk and Galtung), Buzan is usually credited with having got the security debate ball rolling by arguing that 'a notion of security bound to the level of individual states and military issues is inherently inadequate' and that 'the concept of security is, *in itself* [emphasis added], a more versatile, penetrating and useful way to approach the study of international relations than either power or peace' (1991, pp. 3–6).

Despite Buzan's consideration of wider issues, and his contention that 'attempts to treat security as if it was confined to any single level or any single sector invite serious distortion of understanding' (Buzan, 1991, p. 363), his is still very much a realist analysis, albeit a slightly more sophisticated neorealist variant. Far from being radical, he is concerned with the misunderstanding and invective that have become associated with realism and so offers us a more acceptable version that is, nonetheless, concerned primarily with the national security problematic. It would appear that Buzan's ascription of security as an ontological state in itself might explain why his work has been interpreted as so challenging to the orthodox realist view and yet conservative at the same time.

Thus Buzan's work has sent some theorists off on a similar track. The work of Mohammed Ayoob to understand security in the third world can be interpreted in this way (see Ayoob, 1986, 1995). For others Buzan has been an eye-opener but has suggested different directions for research. What is undeniable is that Buzan's work has been a tremendous catalyst in IR's security debate, though paradoxically limiting at the same time, in the sense that it sought to protect, to an extent, the realist position. Perhaps the greatest relevance of Buzan to the debate was his own admission that he is working at a 'high level of abstraction' (1991, p. 374) and that more case-study material is necessary; specific case-study material, of a kind similar to that which informs Chapters 6 and 7, has enhanced understandings of third world security, and is sometimes directly attributable to the work of Buzan (see Pettiford, 1994, 1995).

The work of Ken Booth on security and emancipation (1991a), together with the critical vein of which it forms a part, provides an alternative theoretical position to the work of Buzan. Whilst Buzan's catalyst role is important, his defence of the realist position is susceptible to Booth's criticism that 'if we insist upon old images, the future will naturally tend to replicate the past' (p. 315) – a past of inherent insecurity. Starting from the contention now accepted by most authors that order in world affairs depends on at least minimal levels of political and social justice, Booth seeks to incorporate notions of emancipation into his view of security. He argues that 'true security can only be obtained by people and groups if they do not deprive others of it' (p. 319); this runs counter to the zero-sum logic of security dilemmas (Jervis, 1976). In essence, if security means absence of threat and if emancipation means absence of constraints, then there is a close relationship between them since threat implies constraint and vice versa. In a practical and theoretical sense emancipation *is* security. Booth argues that it is important to go beyond the limited insights of realism/neorealism and that politics is, and should be, rooted in ethics.

If Booth's ideas sound utopian, that is because they unashamedly are. Elsewhere he offers us justification of such a position in Oscar Wilde's observation that 'a map of the world that does not include Utopia is not even worth glancing at' (Booth, 1991b, p. 527). However, Booth talks of process utopianism or utopian realism; this involves an attitude of mind which believes in the possibility of long-term transformation by taking practical steps in the short term. Reminiscent of some environmental thought (see Hayward, 1994 and Chapter 4), Booth argues that 'utopian thinking sets goals and can be a catalyst to action' and in pursuing emancipation the real bases of security can be established (1991b, p. 535). In effect, he argues for putting the individual at the centre of our analysis. However, the question arises of how we could relate these ideas to practical situations; and how this very abstract correlation between security and emancipation might be a useful distinction in isolation from other social, economic and political processes. Some of these epistemological and practical issues with Booth's position will be addressed in Chapter 6.

Another important area which we should draw attention to at an early stage is that of global security. There is an increasingly important body of literature available on the complex processes of globalization, including ever-closer links between individuals, states and societies based on numerous forms of improved communications and travel (see, for example, Featherstone, Lash and Robertson, 1995). These processes have inevitably started to filter into thinking on security and the way in which this has been done has been very varied. Even in a traditional sense, security is having to consider the global spread of high-tech weapons, particularly nuclear proliferation.

However, globalization is having more impact within the security debate, in terms of more recent non-traditional definitions of the concept. Perhaps the most stressed aspects are the threats to humanity posed by potential ecological disaster. Appeals to unity in the face of such threats have, however, been seen as appeals for the third world to help the first maintain its own (excessive) levels of material consumption; for example, Somaya Saad suggests that 'the North has seized control of environmental issues by using them to cloak its own security concerns' (1991, p. 59). The complaint that Western interests have been disguised in global crisis packaging is not a new one, but packaging it in security terms is a more recent phenomenon. Others are working in the area of human rights and the extent to which a universal conception of these is now developing – a debate which has aroused similar anti-Western suspicions. Indeed, globalization has also raised questions related to the ideas of societal and cultural security and how these are being threatened through pressures, amongst others, placed on countries to integrate into the international economic system as well as for communities at the 'local' level to adapt to changing economic conditions, production conditions and so on.

The Structure of the Book in More Detail

Having outlined the emergence of a security debate as well as some important aspects of it, it is worth reminding ourselves that this book is primarily about the changing security agenda in IR *and* how the old and new agendas have either sought or not sought to incorporate the third world into their analysis. However, this task is a little more complicated since the very idea of the third world is itself being challenged. This is because of a number of factors. The first is the disappearance of the so-called second world of Soviet and Eastern bloc countries; the second is the obvious differentiation between countries said to belong to the third world (for example, Chad and South Korea); the third is the rise of countries traditionally associated with the third world looking to join the first world, accompanied by the long-term decline of others in the first (again, compare South Korea with Portugal); the fourth is the increasing differentiation within states so that 'pockets' of elite affluence are clear in the 'third' and areas of structural poverty typical of the 'first'.

In fact, whether we look strategically, politically, economically, psychologically, technologically or geographically it becomes more and more difficult to be certain about the third world; despite such tentativeness, we may nonetheless have a clear mental image of the third world as a totality, which is often reinforced in the post-Cold War by talk of 'North–South' issues in world politics. Whilst we may assert, as a response, that the third world is constituted by those states with poor aggregate economic statistics and little influence in world politics (so that we could confidently put, say, Honduras, Haiti or Mozambique in this category), it is clear that the third world, like security, can no longer be taken as an unchallenged given (so that we would begin to wonder about how to classify Chile, South Korea or South Africa). Accordingly, Chapter 1 seeks to look in more detail at the third world before we attempt to relate the idea to the theoretical development of security. Rather than offering a precise definition of the third world, the chapter should give us not only an understanding of the debates surrounding it but also an idea of 'Southern' perspectives in IR such that we can see that debates over security and the third world engage with critical perspectives on world politics. This chapter's themes are a crucial foundation to bear in mind when considering how they integrate to key questions in later chapters.

Armed with such background, Chapters 2 to 5 follow the security debate. Chapter 2 looks at realism and neorealism and at their efforts, including those from Strategic Studies and Southern viewpoints, to incorporate the third world into their analysis. The 'straw man' of realist security which we have utilized in this introduction is too easy a target; we must recognize the existence of multiple *realisms* with considerable differences of subtlety and emphasis. Before offering the ideas of more thoroughgoing critiques this is where we start our journey.

Chapter 3 looks at more recent challenges to such realist understandings in the form of what may broadly be termed critical security studies; it will consider the influence of critical theory, postmodernism and various strands of feminist thought associated with both critical theory and postmodernism. The challenges of such post-positivist approaches constitute the so-called 'third debate' in IR; they are frequently regarded with hostility, either as unnecessary and distracting or as some kind of new orthodoxy. We aim to demystify these ideas, with a view to peeling away the invective and rhetoric to discover if such approaches offer valuable tools of analysis when looking at security.

Chapter 4 deals specifically with environmental and ecological issues. As suggested above, there is no set approach to security from an environmental perspective; indeed, realists, neorealists, critical and feminist approaches have all sought to incorporate the environment into their analysis. It is precisely because of the rise of the environment onto the international political, economic and security agendas, and the appropriation of key terms such as sustainable development by vested interests, that the chapter seeks to unravel the various arguments which frequently get lost in rhetoric. How green political thought may clarify our thinking on security issues is our aim rather than establishing criteria for achieving *ecological sustainability* or whatever other name may be given to environmental security. Different foundational eco-philosophies are outlined.

In Chapter 5 we particularly consider the autonomous development of Peace Studies/Research and how the categories it has developed such as positive (rather than negative) peace and structural violence may be considered to be having increasing salience in the broader security agenda of the late millennium. The second half of the chapter looks briefly at the contributions and insights which come from Political Geography. The aim of this chapter is really to suggest that the IR security debate must recognize IR as a multi-disciplinary enterprise and that in thinking about security we may already have expertise that we are failing to apply.

Chapters 6 and 7 are basically an attempt to show how rethinking security and the third world can lead to interesting, hopefully useful, insights. Chapter 6 seeks to explore the neglect of poverty and related issues in IR suggesting the reasons for such neglect and arguing that exploring potential linkages between security and development issues may provide a way forward in terms of an explicitly normative micro-security approach. Chapter 7 offers a critique of the ubiquitous term 'sustainable development', and asks what, if anything, sustainable development can add to a development/security approach. We particularly recommend that these chapters are not read in isolation and are seen as part of the whole book.

Our concluding chapter will involve a summary of the book as well as offering food for thought in terms of personal observations about the state of the security debate and where it might be going. From our perspective at least, IR should engage in people-centred security in the third world by looking at issues such as identity and culture, and the ways and forms in which strategies are organized and struggles are conducted to increase security. For us the theoretical assumptions of realism have dovetailed with modernization theory in the third world and statist, ethnocentric, teleological and meta-theoretical epistemology have justified and promoted value-neutral research based on Western ahistorical and acultural generalizations (this is particularly followed up in Chapter 6). In our opinion, attention should be directed toward micro-level research which is indigenously, culturally and historically specific. Ultimately, and via due consideration of multiple theoretical contributions, we hope that this book can make the case for such an approach, but the emphasis we place on *rethinking* means that these are by no means the only conclusions it is possible to draw.

Notes

1. Confusion is sometimes caused because of the existence of structural realism; in Banks' schema, however, structuralism is basically referring to a range of neo-Marxist and dependency theorists.
2. All sorts of things are thus thrown into the pot. It may be tongue in cheek but Galtung (1982) has suggested that lack of sex might be considered a security threat. This is most worrying given the findings of a survey which suggests that people with higher degrees have least sex! ('Education bad for your sex life', *Guardian*, 15 January 1998.)
3. See the debate between Jabri and Chan (1996) and Hollis and Smith (1996), emanating from Wendt's (1991) review of Hollis and Smith's text, *Explaining and Understanding International Relations*, regarding the relationship between ontology and epistemology in IR and methodological processes in research.

References

Ayoob, M. (1986) *Regional Security in the Third World*. London: Croom Helm.
Ayoob, M. (1995) *The Third World Security Predicament*. Boulder, CO: Lynne Rienner.
Azar, E. and Moon, M. (1988) *National Security in the Third World*. Aldershot: Edward Elgar.
Banks, M. (1985) 'The inter-paradigm debate'. In Light, M. and Groom, A.J.R. (eds) *International Relations: A Handbook of Current Theory*. London: Pinter, pp. 7–26.
Beck, U. (1992) *Risk Society: Towards a New Modernity*. London: Sage.
Booth, K. (1990) *New Thinking about Strategy and International Security*. London: Unwin Hyman.
Booth, K. (1991a) 'Security and emancipation', *Review of International Studies*, 17 (3), 313–26.
Booth, K. (1991b) 'Security in anarchy: utopian realism in theory and practice', *International Affairs*, 67 (3), 527–45.
Buzan, B. (1983) *People, States and Fear: The National Security Problem in International Relations*, 1st edition. Brighton: Wheatsheaf.
Buzan, B. (1991) *People, States and Fear: An Agenda for International Security Studies in the Post-Cold War Era*, 2nd edition. Hemel Hempstead: Harvester Wheatsheaf.

Buzan, B. (1995) 'The present as a historic turning point', *Journal of Peace Research*, 30 (4), 385–98.
Calvert, P. (ed.) (1988) *The Central American Security System: North–South or East–West?* Cambridge: Cambridge University Press.
Campbell, D. (1992) *Writing Security*. Manchester: Manchester University Press.
Carlsnaes, W. (1992) 'The agency–structure problem in foreign policy analysis', *International Studies Quarterly*, 36 (3), 245–70.
Chomsky, N. (1987) *Turning the Tide: US Intervention in Central America and the Struggle for Peace*. Montreal: Black Rose Books.
Deudney, D. (1990) 'Environment and security: muddled thinking', *Bulletin of Atomic Scientists*, 47 (3), 22–8.
Deudney, D. (1991) 'The case against linking environmental degradation and national security', *Millennium*, 19 (3), 461–76.
Dunkerley, J. (1988) *Power in the Isthmus*. London: Verso.
Falk, R. (1978) 'Nuclear policy and world order: why denuclearization', *Alternatives*, 3 (3), 321–50.
Featherstone, M., Lash, S. and Robertson, R. (eds) (1995) *Global Modernities*. London: Sage.
Galtung, J. (1969) 'Violence, peace and peace research', *Journal of Peace Research*, 6 (6), 167–90.
Galtung, J. (1982) *Environment and Military Activity: Towards Alternative Security Doctrines*. Oslo: Universitetsforlaget.
George, J. (1994) *Discourses of Global Politics: A Critical (Re)Introduction to International Relations*. London: Macmillan.
Haas, P. (1989) 'Do regimes matter? Epistemic communities and Mediterranean pollution control', *International Organization*, 43 (Summer), 378–403.
Hayward, T. (1994) *Ecological Thought: An Introduction*. Oxford: Polity Press.
Hollis, M. and Smith, S. (1990) *Explaining and Understanding International Relations*. Oxford: Clarendon Press.
Hollis, M. and Smith, S. (1991) 'Beware of gurus: structure and action in international relations', *Review of International Studies*, 17 (4), 393–410.
Hollis, M. and Smith, S. (1994) 'Two stories about structure and agency', *Review of International Studies*, 20 (2), 241–51.
Hollis, M. and Smith, S. (1996) 'A response: why epistemology matters in international theory', *Review of International Studies*, 22 (1), 111–16.
Jabri, V. and Chan, S. (1996) 'The ontologist always rings twice: two more stories about structure and agency in reply to Hollis and Smith', *Review of International Studies*, 22 (1), 107–10.
Jervis, R. (1976) *Perception and Misperception in International Politics*. Princeton: Princeton University Press.
Keohane, R. (1989) *International Institutions and State Power: Essays in International Relations Theory*. Boulder, CO: Westview Press.
Koffman, S. (1977) 'An American social science: international relations', *Daedalus*, 106 (3), 41–60.
Kolodziej, E. and Harkavy, R. (1982) *Security Policies of Developing Countries*. Lexington, MA: Lexington Books.

Krause, K. and Williams, M. (1996) 'Broadening the agenda of security studies: politics and methods', *International Studies Quarterly*, 40 (2), 229–54.
Krause, K. and Williams, M. (eds) (1997) *Critical Security: Concepts and Cases*. London: UCL Press.
Lawler, P. (1990) 'New directions in peace research'. In Emy, H. and Linklater, A. (eds) *Australian Perspectives in International Relations*. Sydney: Allen and Unwin, pp. 109–31.
Lippman, W. (1942) *US Foreign Policy*. Boston: Little, Brown.
Lukes, S. (1974) *Power: A Radical View*. Basingstoke: Macmillan.
Maniruzzaman, T. (1982) *The Security of Small States in the Third World*. Canberra: Australian National University.
Morgenthau, H.J. (1978) *Politics among Nations: The Struggle for Power and Peace*, 5th edition. New York: Alfred Knopf.
Mullins, A.F., Jr (1987) *Born Arming: Development and Military Power in New States*. Stanford: Stanford University Press.
Pasha, M.K. (1996) 'Backlash grows against globalization', *Third World Economics*, No. 145, 635–56.
Pettiford, L. (1994) *Redefining Security in Central America*. University of Southampton: PhD thesis.
Pettiford, L. (1995) *Is That What You Fought the War For? Redefining Security in Central America*. Nottingham Trent University: Politics Occasional Paper Series.
Poku, N. and Pettiford, L. (eds) (1998) *Redefining the Third World*. London: Macmillan.
Rweyemamu, J.F. (1992) *Third World Options: Power, Security and the Hope for Another Development*. Dar es Salaam: Tanzania Publishing House.
Saad, S. (1991) 'For whose benefit? Redefining security', *Eco-Decisions*, September, 59–60.
Saurin, J. (1996a) 'Globalization and poverty in South Asia', *Millennium: Journal of International Studies*, 25 (3), 635–56.
Saurin, J. (1996b) 'Globalization, poverty and the promises of modernity', *Millennium: Journal of International Studies*, 25 (3), 657–80.
Schoultz, L. (1987) *National Security and United States Policy toward Latin America*. Princeton: Princeton University Press.
Smith, S. (1995) 'The self-images of a discipline: a genealogy of international relations theory'. In Booth, K. and Smith, S. (eds) *International Relations Theory Today*. Cambridge: Polity Press, pp. 1–37.
Thomas, C. and Saravanamuttu, P. (1987) *In Search of Security: The Third World in International Relations*. Brighton: Wheatsheaf.
Tickner, J.A. (1995) 'Re-visioning security'. In Booth, K. and Smith, S. (eds) *International Relations Theory Today*. Cambridge: Polity Press, pp. 175–97.
Walt, S. (1991) 'The renaissance of security studies', *International Studies Quarterly*, 35 (2), 211–37.
Weiss, J. and Kessler, M. (1991) *Third World Security in the Post-Cold War Era*. Boulder, CO: Lynne Rienner.
Wendt, A. (1991) 'Bridging the theory/meta-theory gap in international relations', *Review of International Studies*, 17 (4), 383–92.
Williams, P. (1992) *Dilemmas of World Politics: International Issues in a Changing World*. Oxford: Clarendon Press.
Wolfers, A. (1962) *Discord and Collaboration*. Baltimore: Johns Hopkins University Press.

1

Rethinking the Third World

This is, in effect, a second introductory, or foundational, chapter. In the Introduction itself, the idea of security and of how it is being understood in different ways in International Relations (IR) has been outlined; as well as leading into other chapters on *exactly* how security might be rethought or newly understood, or at least what theoretical tools we have for doing so, it also implies that caution is now needed when dealing with the term. This chapter argues that how the words 'third world' are understood should also be the subject of scrutiny: that there is the same need for caution with regard to this term. Though it may *seem* obvious, or in some ways common sense (see Tooze, 1997) (as indeed security was regarded), it certainly bears some critical attention. Whilst the term cannot be regarded as ever having been wholly satisfactory, a variety of contemporary reasons give us further cause for concern (see Poku and Pettiford, 1998), especially if the notion of 'third world security' is to mean anything.

Thus, in talking about changing security agendas *and* the third world it is important to note that this is not simply a case of applying an evolving concept of security in relation to a static idea of the third world. The idea of a third world too needs to be critically re-evaluated if we are to have a fuller picture of its own complexity and a more useful idea to use in the context of the security debate. The concepts of security and of the third world have developed in both separate and intertwined literature in IR. The desire to consider them in practical contexts and around *newer* security issues requires an understanding not only of the benefits of commonality in analysis, but also about how ideas around security and the third world have been constituted in particular political contexts within the discipline and in the international arena. Thus the construction of the third world has been both a construction of history and a history of this construction within IR literature. The idea of the third world as contentious does not prevent us from wanting to focus on third world security in a particular way.

The book as a whole should then be read with a clear appreciation of *which* third world; that is, which kind of state, community or society are we really dealing with as our *referent* of security in any given context? For instance, if neorealism (or at least some neorealist authors) provides us with the tools with which to go beyond the study of great powers and to consider third world *states*, is this actually sufficient for looking at security in the third world or might 'third world security' entail more than this?

The importance of this task stems from the clear idea, intuitively held perhaps, that many people (at least those who consider themselves not to live in it) feel they have about what constitutes the third world. It is one of a whole series of pejorative terms, including 'underdeveloped' or 'developing state' and 'emerging nation', not to mention more overtly offensive terms such as 'uncivilized', 'backward' and 'primitive'. Such terms have tended to be used to *imply* inferiority when compared with others such as 'developed', 'industrialized' or 'first world' which suggest civilization, progress, modernity and, implicitly, superiority. Accordingly, especially through media representation and reinforcement, we have an idea of those countries which we include as 'third world' largely on the basis of generalized poverty (India, Chad and Nicaragua, for instance), and those which we would not. Examples of the latter might be Japan, Italy or the United States. However, even at this stage, we can begin to see problems of categorization in the sense that poverty might well be regarded as 'generalized ' in the United States, southern Italy or parts of Nottingham, for example.

Intuition, common sense or media stereotyping notwithstanding however, and as Naipaul has argued, the internal diversity of what is known as the 'third world' is such that its existence can be no more than mythical; 'there is,' he argues, 'no such thing as the third world' (1995, p. 9). And so, much like a star, the concept should be studied obliquely since under direct observation it appears to dissolve so readily that one questions whether it was ever really there (Norwine and Gonzalez, 1988, p. 2). So, despite our intuitive feelings, perhaps more accurately the images fed from an early age, particularly in the Western media, many students come to question this dichotomous understanding in which it is *states* which fit into one category or the other (first or third world) and where very occasionally a state might justify reclassification.

Such questioning and rejection of simple categorizations comes from a variety of sources, of which this chapter offers a consideration. The sources of dissatisfaction include etymological reasoning; a rejection of the simplicity of the idea and of the categories; a questioning of the belief in modernization and its associated theory and therefore the *stage* of development that *third* world implies; and an uncomfortableness with the ethnocentrism inherent in the whole development discourse[1] (when it is evident that much traditional wisdom has been destroyed by so-called *civilization*, the inferiority/superiority idea is hard to sustain).

This raises the question to what extent we understand the third world as a dialectical construction, with self/other dichotomies led primarily by the epistemological legacy of modernization theory, or as a category which can be defined in and of itself, with boundaries which, albeit with grey areas, clarify where states belong in the hierarchy and why. Certainly, the structuralist literature in IR imported ideas into the discipline which enabled a type of dialectical comparison between the first and the third worlds through ideas of core and periphery, dependency and underdevelopment and, in later work, semi-peripheralization. Whilst the social construction position in IR accounts for the way in which, through discourse, self and otherness, and the third world, are constantly changing and reconstituting themselves, the book retains a core notion of the marginal in order to develop how security is relevant and significant for the discipline at the community and individual levels.

In order, then, to begin a detailed reconsideration of the third world this chapter will look briefly at the evolution of the term itself. Here we initially note the etymological origins of 'third world' in the French language; since the French words *troisième* and *tiers* both mean *third*, which has a double meaning in English, this is both something which needs explanation and something which is often forgotten. We then go on to contextualize the third world in historical and disciplinary contexts and provide the necessary background for exploring a variety of reasons for potential dissatisfaction with the term as it is conventionally understood in IR. We conclude by suggesting that this book, whilst it relates security to the third world in different ways, can be read as an argument for applying the term 'security' most profitably to a notion of third world as those voices marginalized and silenced by IR, rather than 'third world' as simply a collection of rather diverse, but poor, states[2] (see particularly Chapters 3 and 6 for elucidation). This does not indicate a lack of awareness of the ambiguities of the term as it relates to the state level of analysis, but that this notion of the third world remains consistent with the book's main aims and arguments.

To further contextualize/justify our approach, rather like security itself, there is a great deal of power and powerful imagery surrounding the third world. Accordingly, it might be considered ill-advised (or impossible!) simply to shelve it and, therefore, more appropriate to re-examine it critically and see it for its complexity rather than to seek metatheoretical simplicity and generalization.[3] That is the line taken here. Whilst the 'third world' has come to imply certain negative images and resonances to many in the 'first world', being largely descriptive, from the outset we need to remember that the term has become more than *simply* a definition. 'Third world' has come to represent an ideology and a forceful moral position;[4] it does not simply describe the poor, it explains the structural injustice of poverty and prescribes an escape route from it. From the outset then we can see that, outside Western scholarship, 'third world' has transcended the idea of socio-economic categorization, and entails a psychological condition which encompasses the hopes and aspirations – one might add the accumulated bitterness – of the vast majority of humanity (Haas, 1956). Before looking at how we might rethink the third world we need to look at some elements of its existence as a term.

Evolution of 'Third World'

In Language

Whilst recognizing the term's moral strength and physical expression in groups such as the Non-Aligned Movement (NAM), in academic parlance the term 'third world' first appeared in French as *Tiers État*, literally translating as 'Third State' but actually drawing an analogy with pre-revolutionary France. It means those strata of society not belonging to the privileged groups of that particular society, that is, the nobility and the clergy.

Thus in its original conception, whilst not signifying an *exact* fraction, third world means that portion of the population which is under-privileged and marginalized from the upper echelons of society. In some senses this notion has survived, reflecting, during the Cold War, the objective reality of a bipolar (superpower) world. However, the pejorative rather than the descriptive element of third world (positional rather than fractional) seems to have taken over, not least in IR scholarship, where obsession with the ideological struggle between first and second worlds saw the third world marginalized in analysis as much as in reality; a nasty, peripheral arena where they pray to strange gods, important not for itself, but for the first and second worlds' struggle for influence there. Whilst we do not have time to go into such matters here, this highlights issues related to the power of language and the difficulties and importance of translation; for our purposes we can see that one initial objection to the term 'third world' relates to how it has come to be used pejoratively relative to the initial descriptive qualities of *Tiers État*.

As Stereotype

On the concrete issue of what might actually constitute the third world, in the common-sense view we have alluded to, there is a tendency towards some commonality. Sheikh Ali, for instance, contends that the appellation is *used* to refer to 'a non-cohesive group of economically underdeveloped countries located in Asia, Africa and Latin America' (quoted in Poku and Pettiford, 1998, p. 25). Its membership is commonly assumed to be loosely based on a number of characteristics, especially low per capita income, high rates of illiteracy, agriculturally based economies, low degrees of social and actual mobility, short life expectancies, a strong attachment to tradition and a shared historical experience of colonial rule and imperial subjugation. It is this 'accepted' or 'common-sense' view of the third world, frequently backed by a range of pejorative labels, which is becoming unacceptable for a wide range of reasons (see Poku and Pettiford, 1998).

At this point we should note that this image of third worldness as powerlessness caused the almost complete marginalization of the third world in *Western* IR analysis, which is obsessed by state power. However, this image also underpinned structuralist literature, which introduced ideas of core (industrialized North), semi-periphery (in the case of Immanuel Wallerstein's work) and periphery (developing South) into IR. Structuralists have emphasized how the structural economic relations between core and periphery, in the international political economy, are unequal and exploitative. Whilst security has not been the focus of their analysis, this critical approach to the structural location of the third world presented a critique of the dominant paradigm of realism.

Thus, while it is fair to say that third world security was marginalized from conventional IR analysis, the third world itself, though somewhat lumped together in the process, featured prominently in the structuralist literature which was influential in IR theory and practice and development debates from the early 1940s. The term emerged in relation to a group of social scientists at the United Nations Economic Commission for Latin America (ECLA), headed by Raul Prebisch, which concentrated their studies on the economic problems of Latin America. They were concerned with the peripheral position of Latin America in the international economy compared to Western capitalist countries, and 'the heterogeneous structure of the Latin American economies, which were characterized by very uneven levels of development between different sectors' (Jenkins, 1992, p. 136). Structuralism came to be associated with broader social scientific interests, particularly economics, and was based on the assumption that the economic structure of developing states had certain special features which seriously weaken the explanatory power of orthodox economic analysis.

Whilst beginning as a critique of orthodox economic development theory, the structuralist approach came under attack from within its own school and from a revival of neo-liberal economic ideas. Dependency theory, within which there are a number of different strands, focused on the failure of structuralism's import substitution policies whilst the basic needs approach, exemplified by the work of Hans Singer and Dudley Seers, concentrates on the growing inability of economic growth to address inequality and poverty.

Significantly, the focus of the third world's structural location in the international economy highlighted and increased third world countries' awareness of their position, facilitating action to increase their own power and voice in the interational state system. Whilst the third world remained largely excluded from bipolar decision-making structure throughout the Cold War, where politics was fought out by proxy in third world indigenous conflicts such as in Afghanistan and Vietnam, the countries did achieve a level of actorness through demands for a new international economic order (NIEO) and through groupings such as the NAM and the Group of 77 (G77).

As Object of Security

What we will argue for later is active contemplation about the security/third world relationship. We do not suggest that we are the first to consider such a link; from the 1980s there emerged a distinct body of literature in the discipline concentrating specifically on third world security, which went beyond the purely superpower centric approach (see Kolodziej and Harkavy, 1982; Weiss and Kessler, 1991). These approaches concentrated on the strategic location and utility of third world countries within the international system but within a largely post-Buzanian realist framework (Ayoob, 1986, 1995; Alagappa, 1988; Al-Mashat, 1985; Azar and Moon, 1988; Ball, 1988). Another strand of this literature emphasized a non-realist agenda of social, environmental and material problems experienced by third world countries set in the wider context of international relations (see particularly Thomas and Saravanamuttu, 1987; also Thomas, 1992; Pettiford, 1996).

Ayoob's particularly influential work on third world security clearly saw state-building as the main stepping stone to regime stability and therefore security. Basing his analysis on how the Western system of states achieved regime stability and security over centuries of state-building measures, Ayoob argues that third world state behaviour must be understood in the context of the state-making process in which it is involved and the third world's late entry into the postcolonial system of states. Emphasis on political state-making thus underpins the state-centric and political definition of security and contrasts markedly with the proposed analysis of third world states as suggested by Bayart below. Security and therefore national security interests are defined by the political realm. Other security inputs and areas of human and social activity, such as community movements, ecological and economic concerns, are only acknowledged when they threaten state boundaries, political institutions or governing regimes (Ayoob, 1995).

Blurring of the Category

With time the categories of inclusion and exclusion in the category 'third world' have become more contentious and the notion, never entirely without its critics, has become almost highly contested (see Toye, 1987). Bayart argues, for example, that despite the conflict between modernization and dependency theory, both explanations of underdevelopment are based on the belief that external factors have been responsible for political change in Africa, Latin America and Asia since Western colonial expansion. It is argued that this emphasis on external factors (tradition versus modern, core versus periphery) has resulted in a lack of attention to the 'unity and specificity of the economic and political problems' in these continents, and has led to the fantasy of the 'third world' and an over-emphasis on a modern state model based on Western bureaucracy. Third world states' alienation from this norm is 'held responsible for most of the problems associated with political underdevelopment'. Bayart suggests that analysis of third world societies should be based on the 'multiple procedures whereby states are individually created' and the 'long duration' idea where a state's historical trajectory allows modern politics to be placed in its historical context (Bayart, 1991, p. 51).

These practical problems and inherent criticisms are outlined below with the aim of emphasizing that we cannot just redefine or newly understand security and assume that we can throw this new 'blanket' over the third world (some of the newer approaches to security do not, in any case, come in this form). Instead, this idea, the 'third world', itself must be challenged and greater sophistication in analysis of it is surely called for (see Poku and Pettiford, 1998). In doing so, we can then refer to the notion of third world throughout the book with the reader aware of a potentiality of multiple meanings. However, as our conclusions to this chapter will make clear, our own preoccupation is with considering the third world not as a group of states nor *necessarily* as those individuals in absolute poverty (that is, receiving annual incomes of less than a certain amount) but as those who are in some sense marginalized and disempowered in global politics. This need not include those without cash income (see Anderson, 1997).[5]

We now move on to provide some historical background leading to a more detailed discussion of the reasons why we might want to rethink the third world.

Changing Patterns and Differentiation in International Relations

The Cold War dominated post-Second World War IR and world politics (see Mason, 1997, for historical detail of the Cold War itself).[6] It represented a striking instance of a stereotypical political division of labour and, in each of the parallel universes (East and West), one country monopolized political decisions through a variety of inducements, coercion and, occasionally, force. For the most part political analysis assumed it sufficient to judge behaviour on the basis of which camp a given *state* ideologically belonged to, and academic endeavour took the struggle to be pivotal to almost everything about IR. The ideological conflict was characterized by mutual fear, exacerbated by attempts to disrupt each other's camp. In this world, entities as different as Mozambique, Nicaragua and Romania could be viewed as communist, with South Korea, Guatemala and Greece as free world or imperialist. Cold War domination seemed to obstruct IR, so keeping it as the 'backward discipline' (George, 1994)[7] and saw countries easily pigeonholed as either communist or capitalist. These two systems basically competed to demonstrate the superiority of their system to the countries of the third world.

Indeed, Escobar (1995) argues that from 1945 to 1955, during the time when the United States was consolidating its political and economic power, the Marshall Plan was not extended to the third world, which had instead to seek private investment 'to develop'. The 'right climate' for economic growth (development) required for private investment thus imbued the modernization project with a political agenda to curb nationalism, the left, the peasantry and the working class in third world countries. The Cold War was, Escobar argues, 'undoubtedly one of the single most important factors at play in the conformation of the strategy of development. The historical roots of development and those of East–West politics lie in one and the same process: the political rearrangements that occurred after World War Two' (1995, p. 34).

A key intersection of these rearrangements was the fear that poverty and social unrest in the postwar period would pose a threat to the developed world. Another significant occurrence in this period was the 'discovery of the poor' and the rise of ways to intervene, technologically, in health, education, hygiene, morality and so on. It has been argued that the discovery of poverty and the 'transformation of the poor to the assisted' (Escobar, 1995, p. 22) had profound consequences for relations between the industrialized, largely Western countries and the third world. The new social problem of the poor required increasing intervention in society and significantly it was through such intervention that 'in relation to poverty the modern ways of thinking about the meaning of life, the economy, rights and social management came into place' (Escobar, 1995, p. 22; see also Polanyi, 1944). Luke (1991), Dubois (1990) and Crush (1995) link the problematization of poverty to how modernization practices and thought were exported to the third world and how these ideas were clearly linked to US dominance and power. This shift in relations between the postcolonial world and the developed West, on the basis of poverty, is one site where we can clearly see the links between the disciplines of IR and Development Studies (see Rahnema, 1991 and Kothari, 1993). These connections will be explored further in Chapter 6.

Likewise, the end of the Cold War has brought about changes for the third world, for its strategic location both in the international system and in IR analysis. Without detailing the reasons for the end of the Cold War, Francis Fukuyama's thesis in *The End of History and the Last Man* (1992) is an interesting triumphalist view of the implications of its ending.[8] To Fukuyama, the end of the Cold War has signalled that historical alternatives to economic liberalism, and electoral democracy as its natural accompaniment, have become irretrievably discredited or irredeemably unfashionable. Thus, with liberal capitalism now unopposed, as the only remaining ideology of universal validity, the future can only consist of its spread, albeit with minor setbacks. However, this Kantian vision, liberally sprinkled with references to progressive enlightenment optimism has had to contend with international realities which stubbornly refuse to fit into any such teleological scheme; without complete disorder, we now inhabit a world in which growing tensions are nonetheless noticeable. Once rigidly bounded and hysterically concerned with impermeable boundaries, international society (and the analysis of it) has changed so that territorial, ideological and issue boundaries are attenuated, unclear and confusing (Jowitt, 1995, p. 10). We inhabit a world which appears flaky, transient and fragmented, one which is most certainly lacking in Fukuyaman certainty about the inevitable triumph of capitalist democracy and universal freedom.

The changes which are occurring are compounding and exposing ambiguities associated with the orthodoxy of dividing the world into three. This is not simply because of the disappearance of the second world since, as explained above, the 'third world' certainly acquired significance separate from its association with first and second worlds. From the perspective of developing countries, even the idea of a *strategically* bipolar world was itself a distortion; for example, the Chinese Revolution was a very powerful influence, particularly in East and Southeast Asia. In fact, for the vast majority of third world states, the issue never was one of finding a third way between capitalism and communism but of finding a way to operate successfully which preserved some independence from the countries of the developed world.[9]

Thus, contrary to the way it has often been perceived in orthodox IR, the third world was 'not just a group of new states joined later by the older states of Latin America, nor the majority of the world of poor states, but a political alternative other than that presented by Washington and Moscow, the first and second worlds' (Harris, 1990, p. 18). For this reason Kwame Nkrumah has suggested that the third world is neither practical political concept nor reality and that the term has come to mean everything and nothing. To an extent, then Naipaul, referred to earlier, is right to describe the third world as mythical; it is an abstraction or mental construction and it is, in this way, similar to numbers as an extremely useful figment of the human imagination (Boulding, 1980). Thus the 'third world' is at once intellectual, metaphysical and experiential; whilst not actually existing, it is nonetheless encapsulating an ideal — a psychological condition.

What the above suggests is that many of the certainties of orthodox IR scholarship were not, in fact, certainties — at least not outside a very narrow band of intellectual endeavour. It also suggests that now is an absolutely appropriate time to give some detailed and critical consideration to how exactly we might think about the third world within contemporary IR scholarship.

Reasons for Rethinking the Third World

Some might claim that the categorizations offered in looking at the 'third world' are not useful at all; that ultimately all human beings live in and experience the same reality, are governed by the same laws, and that a universal prescription exists for solving the problems of humanity. In particular, the neoliberal messiahs who proclaim such a bright future should be invited to look around, and not simply as their plane is landing and not simply at highly selective examples.[10]

One obvious criticism aimed at the idea of a third world is that since the end of the Cold War the 'second world' has ceased to exist. As will have been seen above, 'third world' itself has travelled the road from meaning 'a (disadvantaged) third of the world' to a more usual understanding as 'the world in third place'; the pejorative implications of this latter meaning could only be emphasized and reinforced by promoting the 'third world' into second place but it is a logical objection to the term.[11]

Despite problems with ordering countries, and the tendency to do this on the basis of gross national product (GNP), some do, however, argue that the vast differentiation amongst countries of the third world means that more categories are called for, that having three worlds is overly simplistic. They argue that a threefold global socio-economic stratification is much too simplistic to reflect a vast diversity of cultures, economies and values. Exactly how many categories there should be is debated and various typologies might be suggested (see, for example, Chan, 1998; Quadir and Shaw, 1998). Indeed, some literature already makes effective distinctions between less developed countries (LDCs) and least developed countries (LLDCs). Furthermore, there are a whole series of newly industrializing countries (NICs) with enormously varying GNPs, including on a per capita basis, and various other existing categories which it would be possible to make use of.

In looking to pigeon-hole the nations of the world in this way, it is also worth noting that some (so-called) third world countries have weight, influence or presence in international politics by virtue of their size, such as China, India, Indonesia or Brazil. However, others have been so dominated by foreign powers throughout their history so as to have little influence; examples are Nicaragua and Laos. How are we to classify these states? Indeed, should we attempt to? And what about nominal players in the international system, such as Chad, where the state has virtually or actually ceased to exist in any meaningful sense at all?

Problems with any such state-based characterizations or typologies are exemplified by the use of GNP or gross domestic product (GDP) per capita as the defining economic indicator of development. One important function of economic statistics such as GNP is to establish a structure in which states can be measured and compared in relation to the industrialized West. This way of categorizing and evaluating a state's development is coming increasingly into question for a variety of reasons, and in the process questions are inevitably raised about the term 'third world' itself. Does GNP really represent the most appropriate way to classify states? Since GNP includes destruction and depletion of assets,[12] as well as production, and excludes any notion of distribution, is it an accurate or desirable method of measuring 'progress' either economically or environmentally? Are not development statistics 'techno-representations endowed with complex political and cultural histories' which cannot be accessed through a narrow statistical framework? (See Escobar, 1995, p. 213.) Furthermore, one wonders if, given examples such as South Korea and Portugal, it really is helping to break down imaginings of what constitutes the first and third worlds in this way; or if, indeed, our imaginings may stay still long after these figures change.

Perhaps the most serious objection to the idea of GNP is its links to modernization economics, underpinned by modernization theory's assumptions about how best to move out of poverty. Modernization theory, in its various forms (economic, sociological, political),[13] represents ultimate faith in 'development', understood as the discourse through which the developed, civilized West represents the destination for 'underdeveloped' third world states. Binary oppositions in common usage, such as developed/underdeveloped, advanced/backward and civilized/uncivilized, became infused in development thinking through the teleological construction of modernization. At any time states may be placed on the development ladder – some may not be doing terribly well at this particular time, but 'developed' is where all states are heading, or can head, given the right amount of 'expert' assistance. Rostow's stages of growth theory (1960) is an example of how the economic and political aspects of modernization theory coalesced.

In order to judge just how far down the road any given third world state is, we need only look at its figures for GNP per capita. As suggested, there are some very practical ecological reasons for being unhappy with this way of thinking (see Chapter 4). There are also some moral and cultural objections to supposing that there is only one way to do things; the implication is almost that we will one day all sit down together for a TV dinner, watch *The Simpsons* and drink Coke or Budweiser, and that this is desirable/inevitable. The idea that certain material possessions symbolize the achievement of a particularly Western lifestyle is also informed by the suggestion of 'growth as development'. Furthermore, empirical observation just does not bear out the optimism of development; Rist (1997) compares it to a religion whose practitioners continue to believe because of apparent miracles such as South Korea, despite the social and ecological consequences and despite some of the heretical methods used along the way.

Though we have not seen a continuously growing gap between *all* rich and *all* poor countries in recent decades we have most certainly not seen an uncomplicated succession of take-offs as modernization theory had predicted.[14] Furthermore, the gap between the richest people and the poorest people *is* growing in both relative and absolute terms.

GNP has often been isolated from other relevant factors in overly economistic analysis of development. Of course, viewing GNP as the only relevant development indicator is inappropriate, but when viewed in conjunction with other social indicators such as infant mortality, literacy and health, it *can* provide evidence of changes in material conditions of existence which may be useful in certain contexts. Dudley Seers is one of the most prominent critics of the economic definition of development which emphasizes productivity, growth at social cost and increasing GNP as the primary development goal. His human needs' approach (Seers, 1969) put forward the idea that development must first start with ensuring the conditions for achievement of as Seers puts it, 'the realization of the potential of human personality' rather than from production and growth (quoted in Thomas and Potter, 1992, p. 121). The first three conditions – the capacity to obtain physical necessities; a job (not necessarily paid employment); and equality, an objective in its own right – argued against the economistic view of development which did not necessarily alleviate poverty. Seers argued that 'from a long-term viewpoint, economic growth is for a poor country a necessary condition of reducing poverty. But it is not a sufficient condition. To realise the development potential of a high rate of economic growth depends on policy' (1992, p. 121). Seers' argument highlighted the growth versus equity component in development debates which recognized the inability of GNP to measure inequality which could stem from economic development (see Thomas and Potter, 1992, pp. 121–4).

GNP as an indicator of development is therefore also unsatisfactory, and this relates directly to debates over the usefulness of the third world, because it is based on states (and in this sense congruent with a hierarchical realist world-view which suits the *tiering* of first, second and third worlds). The changing nature and spatial distribution of poverty under pressure from the forces of globalization must surely challenge a state-based, geographical notion of the third world; the geographical ring-fencing of most typologies is increasingly challenged by contemporary patterns of global politics. If we take China as an example, we see many different and almost separate worlds: some, such as Shanghai, are characterized by urban growth, dynamism and conspicuous consumption (as well as crime, poverty and other social problems), others, in the interior, by environmental degradation and grinding rural poverty. Similarly, in all countries of the world we can see huge disparities of wealth and other social indicators; the capital city of the world's most powerful country, Washington, DC, in the United States, has an average life expectancy of 62, which is comparable with much of the third world. As mobile capital chases the cheapest labour, living in the first world and being unskilled is not a nice position to be in.[15] Furthermore, ostentatious wealth can be seen in cities all over the world. Of course, the causal linkages between the worlds of the rich and the

Rethinking the Third World 35

poor are definable, but how can we draw lines round countries and allocate third world status when such startling differentiations of wealth exist even within the exemplars *par excellence* of first and third worlds?

Thus what we now have is a complex global politico-economic system which has, at least as far as states are concerned, superseded and problematized the old simplicities of a world divided into a series of dichotomous categories such as 'first/third, rich/poor, civilized/uncivilized, haves/have-nots and industrialized/agrarian' (see Harris, 1990). What this all suggests to us, in thinking about security in a third world context, is not the need for a new group of categories by which the third, fourth, fifth, sixth and so on worlds may be delineated, nor for some more sophisticated colouring scheme whereby the interior of China is a different colour from the condominiums of Rio de Janeiro and perhaps the same colour as the *favelas* of Rio and areas of Liverpool, Athens or Madrid. What it *does* suggest is coming to terms with a changing pattern of international relations and adapting our thinking on security accordingly; it suggests rejecting the image of the third world as a Weberian 'ideal type' of poverty, political cleavages, low economic clout and poor political prestige in favour of greater complexity in analysis. In terms of the third world, greater complexity means a rejection of state-based imagery and a critical/reflective approach; in terms of (third world) security we need to be clear about what security means, for whom or what, and what the implications might be of securitizing issues in particular ways. This is an important project for international relations; to explore what critical means in practice, and what utility discussions around critical security or emancipatory security in IR have for marginalized and poor people who inhabit the third world. To propose an emancipatory politics is not necessarily to emancipate. Again, we do not provide an answer to this puzzle but suggest that it requires thought throughout the book.

In this sense, whether or how to redefine the third world becomes not a task to be accomplished but an open-ended question and site for academic debate. In any case, the third world needs rethinking. In relating the third world to security it becomes not just a question of exposing the reasons why third world *states* were excluded, and then trying to include them, but thinking about whom and what else is excluded and how this might be included. The third world, despite the problems with the term and its pejorative connotations, remains a potent symbol of the marginalized and oppressed; whilst the project to 'dispel the third world as myth' is helpful and necessary to identify how the term is neither coherent nor holistic, we do not deny the massive material disparities that remain in a very real way between the third and first worlds. However, to the extent that it has frequently been co-opted by those doing the oppression, it needs to be reclaimed by the oppressed and, in this context, re-understood as a tool of analysis for IR scholars.

Conclusions

What the foregoing has sought to do, as much as anything else, is raise a whole series of *questions* about an idea which has been seen as almost self-evident by scholars and, especially, policy-makers. In this sense at least, 'third world' is very similar to security. However, it is unlike security in the sense that we may wish to *untie* security from its realist roots, whereas with the third world it is more a case of going back to its roots.

From a critical perspective 'third world' is, in a way, similar to Marxism; some of the emotional elements in the idea (its value as a mobilizer of anti-colonial, emancipatory ideals) may be considered worth preserving, especially as they relate to newer definitions of security. This is not least because they keep us alert, throughout any intellectual probing we may do, to the real material inequalities which exist throughout the world (Escobar, 1995). By the time the concluding chapter of this book is reached, it is hoped that readers will be in a position to make this decision for themselves.

The questions raised here are largely left as such in an effort to emphasize the possibility of different conceptions of 'third world' as well as different notions of security. As we assess changing security agendas and the third world we are looking for more complex and considered analysis which shuns over-simplified categorizations. Whilst it is not necessary to repeat here detailed discussion of the methodology which might be employed in such an endeavour (see Poku and Pettiford, 1998), what is attempted as we work through the book is a demonstration of how the ways in which security is re-defined and re-understood have the potential for different levels of significance when applied to *different* third worlds. We ultimately argue that in marginalized communities throughout the globe and in the strategies of resistance they offer, frequently in an ecological context, to mediate and cope with the consequences of neo-liberal globalization, we can see a profitable way to understand a nexus in which the third world is seen as marginalized and security as a goal which is actively sought through various strategies.

In reaching such conclusions this book next seeks to work through key developments in the security debate as a part of IR more generally. In demonstrating key thinking in the discipline and surrounding security, we hope to position those arguments made in Chapters 6 and 7, as well as in the concluding chapter, and to strengthen them as a result. As we have stressed earlier, the later chapters cannot be seen as a logical end-point; however, they can be seen as the ways we have chosen to think through some of the problematiques raised by this book's consideration of 'third world' and 'security'.

We now move on to show how security has been subject to a series of reinterpretations by various theorists which, added together, form the basis of the security debate within the discipline. Much of this debate has been conducted in fairly acrimonious terms, and as an either/or dichotomy. Whilst the positions presented here are quite different, and should stimulate thoughts on the way to understand security, and though the debate has been increasingly polemic (see Walt, 1991 and Hansen, 1997), we doubt the need for such polemics; having presented various reformulations of security, and despite *preferences* in terms of how to understand security, the need for an either/or debate, as opposed to a more constructive process of critical engagement, is also addressed in our conclusions.

Notes

1. A discourse might be defined as a 'matrix of social practices that gives meaning to the way that people understand themselves and their behaviour [thus] generat[ing] the categories of meaning by which reality can be understood and explained' (George, 1994). In effect a discourse means an orthodox or prevailing way of thinking, talking and acting in a certain area (in this case, development) which is not normally stepped outside of by most people.
2. 'Profitably' here could be taken to mean not only in a purely academic sense (that is, by providing new insights), but also in a political sense (that is, by giving voices to the silenced).
3. The methodological implications of this are thoroughly expounded by N. Poku in sections of Poku and Pettiford (1998).
4. See, for example, the politics of Fidel Castro, the poetry of Ame Cesaire or the economics of Mahub ul-haq (Poku and Pettiford, 1998).
5. Arguments are simply explained here surrounding the need to look not at absolute money income levels but at relative deprivation.
6. The distinction here is between disciplinary IR (capitalized) and what actually happens in global politics (lower case). Though this distinction is sometimes confusing, not least because the abbreviation for each is IR, it is felt useful to have such a division when it is important to emphasize one, the other or, as here, both.

7. George argues that IR remained fixed in an entrenched conservatism, so avoiding many influences in social theory which could have avoided the 'silences' so characteristic of the discipline.
8. See also Zakaria (1997), who draws rather a less rosy picture than Fukuyama.
9. Thus Nicaragua did not break away from US domination in order to jump into the Soviet camp. It attempted, and indeed none other than Castro advised it, to transform society without breaking from the West's economic arrangements. Because US/Reagan-administration Cold War paranoia pushed Nicaragua into Soviet dependence, it does not alter the fact that such an alliance was not sought for either strategic or ideological reasons.
10. The tendency to forget the practical problems of the third world is displayed not simply by liberals but by others, such as certain 'deep greens' who in emphasizing 'bioregionalism' or 'wilderness' frequently *seem* to forget the everyday experience of many (see Chapter 4).
11. It could also reinforce progressive/modernization notions which we deal with here as well.
12. For example, should the clean-up from an oil spill really appear as a part of GNP? Does reliance on this figure, and the expectation that it will permanently rise, lead to the short-term sacrifice of assets, such as forest reserves, which could make a more modest but longer-term contribution to national wealth and welfare?
13. For a good introduction to modernization theory, see Larrain (1989).
14. For an excellent and bitterly ironic critique of Rostow, see Baran and Hobsbawm (1973).
15. Despite this argument, we should at least note at this point the tendency for concentrated economic growth in the Triad of North America, Europe and Japan. Whilst certain areas of what has traditionally been known as the third world are tied into this triad, on more or less favourable terms, it is nonetheless the case that many countries (particularly in Africa) are attracting less and less investment.

References

Alagappa, M. (1987) *The National Security of Developing States: Lessons from Thailand*. Dover: Auburn House.
Al-Mashat, A. (1985) *National Security in the Third World*. Boulder, CO: Westview Press.
Anderson, P. (1997) *The International Politics of Power, Justice and Death*. London: Routledge.
Ayoob, M. (1986) *Regional Security in the Third World*. London: Croom Helm.
Ayoob, M. (1995) *The Third World Security Predicament*. Boulder, CO: Lynne Rienner.
Azar, E. and Moon, M. (1988) *National Security in the Third World*. Aldershot: Edward Elgar.
Ball, N. (1988) *Security and Economy in the Third World*. London: Adamantine Press.
Baran, P. and Hobsbawm, E. 'The stages of economic growth: a review'. In Wilber, C. (ed.) *The Development of Underdevelopment*. New York: Random House, pp. 45–54.
Bayart, J. (1991) 'Finishing with the idea of the third world: the concept of the political trajectory'. In Manor, J. (ed.) *Rethinking Third World Politics*. London: Longman, pp. 51–71.

Booth, K. and Smith, S. (1997) *Globalization: An Introduction to International Relations*. Oxford: Oxford University Press.
Boulding, K. (1980) 'Science: our common heritage', Presidential address at the annual meeting of the American Association for the Advancement of Science, San Fransisco.
Chan, S. (1998) 'Redefining the third world for a new millennium: an aching towards subjectivity'. In Poku, N. and Pettiford, L. (eds) *Redefining the Third World*. Basingstoke: Macmillan, pp. 16–23.
Crush, J. (ed.) (1995) *Power of Development*. London: Routledge.
Dubois, M. (1991) 'The governance of the third world: a Foucauldian perspective on power relations in development', *Alternatives*, 16 (1), 1–30.
Escobar, A. (1995) *Encountering Development: The Making and Unmaking of the Third World*. Princeton: Princeton University Press.
Fukuyama, F. (1992) *The End of History and the Last Man*. Ithaca, NY: Cornell University Press.
George, J. (1994) *Discourses of Global Politics: A Critical (Re)Introduction to International Relations*. London: Macmillan.
Haas, W. (1956) *The Destiny of the Mind: East and West*. London: Macmillan.
Hansen, L. (1997) 'A case for seduction? Poststructuralist contributions to the security debate', *Conflict and Cooperation: Nordic Journal of International Studies*, 32 (4), 369–98.
Harris, N. (1990) *The End of the Third World*. Harmondsworth: Penguin.
Jenkins, R. (1992) 'Theoretical perspectives'. In Hewitt, T., Johnson, H. and Wield, D. (1992) *Industrialization and Development*. Oxford: Oxford University Press, pp. 128–66.
Jowitt, K. (1995) 'A world without Leninism'. In Slater, R.O. (ed.) *Global Transformation and the Third World*. Boulder, CO: Lynne Rienner.
Kolodziej, E. and Harkavy, R. (1982) *Security Policies of Developing Countries*. Lexington, MA: Lexington Books.
Kothari, R. (1993) *Poverty: Human Consciousness and the Amnesia of Development*. London: Zed Books.
Larrain, J. (1989) *Theories of Development*. Cambridge: Polity Press.
Luke, T. (1991) 'The discourse of development: a genealogy of "developing nations" and the discipline of modernity', *Social Theory*, 11 (2), 271–93.
Mason, J. (1997) *The Cold War*. London: Routledge.
Naipaul, S. (1995) 'A thousand million invisible men: the myth of the third world', *The Spectator*, 18 May, 9–11.
Norwine, J. and Gonzalez, A. (eds) (1988) *The Third World: States of Mind and Being*. London: Unwin Hyman.
Pettiford, L. (1996), 'Redefining security in the third world', *Third World Quarterly*, 17 (2), 289–306.
Poku, N. and Pettiford, L. (eds) (1998) *Redefining the Third World*. Basingstoke: Macmillan.
Polanyi, K. (1944) *The Great Transformation*. New York: Rinehart.
Quadir, F. and Shaw, T. (1998) 'Southeast Asia in the twenty-first century: human security and regional development'. In Poku, N. and Pettiford, L. *Redefining the Third World*. Basingstoke: Macmillan, pp. 172–98.
Rahnema, M. (1991) 'Globalising poverty: pauperising myth', *Interculture*, 24 (2), 4–51.
Rist, G. (1997) *The History of Development: From Western Origins to Global Faith*. London: Zed Books.

Rostow, W.W. (1960) *Stages of Economic Growth*. Cambridge: Cambridge University Press.

Seers, D. (1969) 'The meaning of development', in Lehmann, D. (ed.) *Development Theory: Four Critical Studies*. London: Frank Cass.

Singer, H. (1989) 'Lessons of post-war development experience: 1945–1988', *Discussion Paper No. 260*, Brighton: Institute of Development Studies, University of Sussex.

Thomas, A. and Potter, D. (1992) 'Development, capitalism and the nation-state'. In Allen, T. and Thomas, A. (eds) *Poverty and Development in the 1990s*. Oxford: Oxford University Press, pp. 116–41.

Thomas, C. (1992) *The Environment in International Relations*. London: Royal Institute for International Affairs.

Thomas, C. and Saravanamuttu, P. (1987) *In Search of Security: The Third World in International Relations*. Brighton: Wheatsheaf.

Tooze, R. (1997) 'International political economy in an age of globalization'. In Bayliss, J. and Smith, S. *The Globalization of World Politics*. Oxford: Oxford University Press, pp. 212–30.

Toye, J. (1987) *Dilemmas of Development*. Oxford: Blackwell.

Walt, S. (1991) 'The renaissance of security studies', *International Studies Quarterly*, 35 (2), 211–37.

Weiss, J. and Kessler, M. (1991) *Third World Security in the Post-Cold War Era*. Boulder, CO: Lynne Rienner.

Zakaria, F. (1997) 'The rise of illiberal democracy'. *Foreign Policy*, 76 (6), 22–43.

2

Opening the Can of Worms: Realism to Neorealism

This chapter is entitled 'Opening the Can of Worms' to suggest that while neorealism retains a profoundly realist state-centric bias, various neorealist authors have made a significant contribution to the security debate. This removal of the lid from a can of worms can be regarded as a starting-point in stimulating thinking about how best to understand the concept of security. Neorealists have, somewhat ironically, helped in moving towards understandings of security which are not state b(i)ased.

In addressing the transition 'realism to neorealism', this chapter seeks first to elaborate a little on realism itself. Realism, no less than other -isms, such as socialism, is not a monolithic point of view. Thus when we go on, to reiterate the realist orthodoxy surrounding the concept of security, it should be borne in mind that here is a research agenda in itself, for those who are so inclined. Our purposes, to suggest the possibilities of rethinking security, are served by the construction of a 'straw man', but it is worth remembering that this is what we do.

Accordingly, the specifics and nuances of how realist analyses have actually considered the third world will *not* be included since we do not consider that they offer very much in terms of how we think about third world security. By this we mean that the work done within a realist framework (strategic studies), whose primary aim was to look at the third world, did so not for itself, but solely in terms of the world balance of power or global correlation of forces. Within such frameworks, the third world was simply a geographical space where Cold War tensions were fought out and where alliances and regional power balances were crucial points of discussion; however, the third world was, in every sense, peripheral to the main debate which was concerned with superpower equilibrium.

Instead, our concentration is on the period from the 1980s onwards when currents within mainstream realist analysis (that is, neorealism) finally seemed to have acquired *some* relevance to the third world itself rather than that of simply being associated with the grander scheme of international relations. Although the third world is still geographically delineated and state based, some neorealist analyses have recognized the necessity of thinking about security in other than great power and military terms. Here we are concerned, again, not with the full breadth of neorealist thinking and writing but with highlighting a way of thinking; we have chosen to discuss selectively the work of those who have helped to open up thinking about security, giving it a relevance beyond the world's most powerful states.

Whilst this chapter involves implicit criticisms of both realist and neorealist approaches, highlighting areas of inadequacy, these are made more explicitly in the chapters which deal with critical, postmodern and ecological approaches to security (Chapters 3 to 5). In other words, before examining the worms, we first look at how and why the can was opened. However, initially we offer some reflections on realism and the realist orthodoxy around security.

Realism or Realisms?

It is an easy trap to fall into but, whether out of pedagogic convenience or theoretical contempt, realism is often dealt with briefly and simplistically in contemporary IR teaching (Pettiford and Poku, 1996). It is reduced to a series of simplified assumptions about actors, interests and processes in world politics which tend to preclude complexity or subtlety of analysis. However, it would be better to regard realism, as, say, Bartleson (1996) does, as a site of contention rather than as a unified position.

The classical view, associated with, for instance, Morgenthau (1978) and Beard (1966), differs from the so-called English school variation of Bull (1977) and Wight (1978) and those who emphasize a Grotian account of the central role of international society. Then there is the structural realism of Waltz (1959, 1979). Some realists can be considered a good deal more self-critical than others and sceptical of many dispositions of realism as it has tended to evolve (Wolfers, 1963). Realists with Marxist and/or Christian backgrounds bring different shades to their work (Carr, 1964; Niebuhr, 1953; also Wight, 1978). And the tendency of realists to carry Cold War baggage and to proclaim the certainty of US liberal positions is less evident in some work (Aron, 1966). This short section draws attention to such differences without exploring them (see Smith, 1986).

We do not consider it our job to entirely correct perceptions of realism as monolithic; realism does, after all, always include power politics, the balance of power and the politics of territoriality as its central concepts or at least as centres of contention. Realism's state-centredness is extremely pervasive. Furthermore, our emphasis in this project would still be the general realist disposition to reductionism in claiming the autonomy of international politics and its neglect of people and their security (or forms of identity) *in relation to* the state. In other words, we can use a general realist position in comparing it with other ways of thinking about security whilst accepting, and being aware of, a number of variations.

'The' Realist Orthodoxy

Theoretical critiques of idealism, such as those of Carr (1964), as well as the experience of the Second World War saw realism emerge after the war as the dominant orthodoxy in IR, with its principles perhaps most ably and lucidly characterized in Morgenthau's classic text *Politics among Nations* and his 'six points' of political realism. In such traditional realism, security is very close to power in its practical significance and 'international politics, like all politics, is a struggle for power' (1978, p. 25). In other words, to be secure a state must have the physical ability to militarily deter attacks and/or repel actual attacks. In effect, the predominance of the realist paradigm in IR led to the meaning of security being subsumed under the rubric of power (see Tickner, 1995, p. 176). Fundamental to a realist view is the timeless nature of security as a unit (state)-based struggle within anarchy, regardless of which particular anarchic system we are talking about (see Thucydides, 1998). Thus Ken Waltz, writing in the late 1950s, suggests that 'it may be true that the Soviet Union poses the greatest threat of war at the present time. It is not true that were the Soviet Union to disappear the remaining states could easily live in peace' (1959, p. 230). Accordingly and ironically, when the Soviet Union did disappear, this was the reason why some Western strategists almost mourned the passing of established patterns and certainties, despite a lifetime of opposing the USSR and its political system.

There is thus a double tragedy in realist security. The first part is that it is ahistorical. This means that the laws of realism are said to be (almost) scientific laws – inescapable like gravitational pull, and valid regardless of historical context, unsusceptible to human ingenuity and progress. Accordingly, the search for absolute security from and within anarchy is unending; this in turn implies a certain hopelessness and limits the search for alternative understandings of what security might be as ultimately futile. The second part of the double tragedy is that realist security is a zero-sum phenomenon; that is, in increasing one's own security, the *in*security of others is also increased. Put simply, more soldiers, guns, tanks and jet-fighters may make a state feel more secure in the short term but, in the longer term, those states made to feel *less* secure by this build-up will conscript more soldiers and manufacture more military hardware in an effort to become more secure. These efforts will make the state which originally built up its military machine feel less secure, demonstrating that its original efforts in seeking security led to only a transient period of security. In other words, security is a constant competition in which a state may feel more or less secure at any given time but where the total amount of security is the same. My gain is your loss and vice versa. This has been described by various authors and is usually referred to as the security dilemma (see Herz, 1950). This dilemma can lead to arms races (in Jervis' terms 'a spiral of insecurity' – see Jervis, 1976 and 1991) and tends towards a position of permanent insecurity in the system as a whole and, at best, only temporary security for any given power at any given time. Indeed, John Vasquez (1983) has convincingly argued that realist power politics promotes certain kinds of behaviour leading to a self-fulfilling prophecy of antagonism between nations.

Within realism's military defensive notions of security the concept of the balance of power is crucial. According to advocates of this idea, weaker military powers will naturally ally in order to balance the superior military power of larger ones, thus preventing imperial domination of the international system by any single power (see Bull, 1977; for a simple introduction, see Berridge, 1992). Such a notion may therefore offer hope for states clearly unable to provide sufficient military power to ensure their own security from attack (that is, those which are too small or which lack sufficient economic resources). However, the balance of power also allows for the possibility that some states may have to be sacrificed in order to maintain an overall balance. Indeed, the aim of the balance is not to prevent all wars but to maintain the international system of states (which is of course highly unequal) and where necessary by war.

It is clear from the outset why such a status quo orientation as realism might have been considered an inadequate tool of analysis by and for the third world. It might be argued that the balance of power *could* be used in regional (third world) contexts; for example, Buzan uses the notion of 'security complexes' which he describes as 'patterns of amity and enmity (between states) that are substantially confined within some particular geographical area' (1991a, p. 190). He argues that national security in the third world is a relative phenomenon that cannot be understood outside the context of the 'international pattern of security interdependence within which it is embedded' (1992, p. 167). As an example, Buzan says that the region of Southeast Asia 'illustrates a relationship among domestic, regional and global security that can be found throughout the third world' (1989, p. 11). As such, Southeast Asian security problems for Buzan are understood within this context. However, before Buzan's appeal for regional case-studies, realists did not occupy themselves with such tasks, since they were already preoccupied elsewhere. In any case, from our point of view, concerns clearly need to go beyond this if any meaningful analysis is to be provided of other than a minority of 'important' states whether these be regional or global great powers.

Realism has thus provided little of value in attempting to study security in third world contexts other than within balance of power, state-based analyses. Its concentration on power and its inherent tendency towards maintaining the status quo has had little to offer to those who are *weak* (states and individuals), that is, those with most to gain from a change in the status quo. By weak we mean lacking in genuine political and economic agency within the international system. It is this latter point, combined with the increasing sophistication of weaponry, such that an ostensibly weak power might acquire a few weapons of mass destruction and hence influence out of proportion to its power, that finally led some realists to consider the third world in their analyses. However, the concern was not with the security of (or for) the third world but with how such states must be carefully controlled given their, we might add *just*, motivations for threatening the security of others. The third world is effectively demonized in such arguments, with its leaders frequently labelled as 'madmen' even when raising legitimate questions of international justice.

As stated in the Introduction, literature which considered third world security only as it related to the overall security of the system will not be dwelt upon, although the creation of external threats through a process of dichotomous thinking is an interesting avenue for further research (see Campbell, 1992). For now it is sufficient to note that realism provided a highly attractive way of looking at security if one were simply to learn lessons of the 1930s and longed for stability rather than senseless slaughter in the world, and particularly in Europe. However, at the time when realism came to dominate (around the time of the Second World War), the third world did not even exist in the sense that it was subsequently to enter conventional discourse; to speak of challenges to the status quo, at that time, seemed to have more to do with Hitlerian attempts at imperial conquest than demands for independence, international equity and social justice by the vast majority of the world's people (Burchill and Linklater, 1996).

Realist justification for the (continued) dominance of power politics was/is not that this theoretical position can account for everything – far from it in fact. Realism admits to being, indeed is sometimes proud of being, an elegant simplification. It is said to be the essence which allows us to understand a complex world. It is not reality, but a tool, rather like economics, which allows us a solid grip on a reality which would otherwise be far too complicated for the human mind to picture. This does not mean that realists themselves are amoral,[1] but that they believe laws of realism are immune to moral injunction. Thus, when Jim George (1994) berates realism by claiming that 'a complex, ambiguous and heterogeneous matrix has been reduced in International Relations intellectual and policy circles to a simplistic, universalised image of the "real" world, which is fundamentally detached from the everyday experience of so much of that world', the full force of this anger is unlikely to be felt in realist circles. The realist might well respond that complexity *must* be reduced in order to aid understanding, that simplicity is in this case elegant and that the world of the states*man* is inevitably divorced from the everyday experience of the vast majority.

For those who have sought to defend traditional approaches, 'given the cost of military forces and the risks of modern wars, it would be irresponsible for the scholarly community to ignore the central [realist] questions that form the heart of the security studies field' (Walt, 1991, p. 213). In the same article, Walt approvingly uses Morgenthau to suggest that 'if security studies succumbs to the tendency for academic disciplines to pursue [in Morgenthau's words] "the trivial, the formal, the methodological, the purely theoretical, the remotely historical – in short, the politically irrelevant"...., its theoretical progress and practical value will increasingly decline' (Walt, 1991, p. 222). It is perhaps ironic that the initial impetus to such 'political irrelevance' (the reference is to what can broadly be termed poststructuralism) seems to have come from within the realist camp itself (see Chapter 3).

Neorealism and Security

Neorealism and neorealist revisions of security are fundamentally a response to perceived changes in the real world and an unhappiness with realism's inflexibility in this context. Thus neorealism is much less coherent a position than even realism, whose neglected variations we have already alluded to. However, though neorealism has developed an increasing awareness of the third world, the increasing salience of economics in international relations and so on, it has, most fundamentally, retained realism's state-centric bias. Neorealism has also been significant in emphasizing structure at the expense of human nature in explaining the (lack of) agency of state actors.

We move now to look at influential neorealist analyses of security whilst bearing in mind the extent to which these bring relevance to realist security in a third world context or serve to preserve its status quo orientation. What we are not attempting here is a thorough survey of the whole spectrum of neorealist thought. What we highlight is the work of particular authors who have served to provide new tools for a consideration of the third world. Others have also done relevant research in this context, but our aim is to provide a useful way into the study of third world security from predominantly state-based perspectives.

Neorealism in IR did not arrive as an attack on the concept of security, rather its ideas and some of its theorists have had influence in provoking the debate in which security has been described as too broadly defined to be of any practical value or at least so contested/vague that confusion is the inevitable result (see Deudney, 1991). Neorealism initially aimed to emphasize the importance of structural factors in explaining international dynamics rather than simply inherent evil in human nature as classical and traditional realist strands had sought to do (see Waltz, 1959). Neorealism also sought to raise the profile of economic factors in the analysis of international relations.

Its significance, in the sense of providing a genuine break with realism, may be put into context by considering the words of Richard Ashley, who argues that neorealism is 'positivist structuralism that treats the given order as the natural order, limits rather than expands political discourse, negates or trivializes the significance of variety across time and place [and] subordinates all practice to an interest in control' (1984, p. 228). The power of such criticism will be explained and evaluated further in the next chapter. For the time being, we leap to neorealism's defence.

By highlighting the constraints of structure and the importance of economics, neorealism can clearly be seen as taking an important step towards greater relevance to the third world. Although there are arguments to the contrary, since neorealism has based its structural approach on the sovereign state-system (for expansion of such arguments, see Wendt, 1991), neorealism's role as a catalyst in moving to non-state-based definitions is less contentious (though nonetheless contended).

As mentioned in the Introduction, perhaps the greatest, or at least first serious, challenge to traditional realist definitions from within realism itself came from neorealist Barry Buzan's *People, States and Fear* (see Buzan, 1983, 1991a). His project is to examine the interaction between different levels of analysis (individual, national and international) leading to constructive re-definitions of security. Crucially, Buzan recognizes (and begins to convince the IR community) not only that security can be issue based (for example, economics and environment) but also that states may not be the only referent object in terms of (in)security. Other actors, such as individuals or nations, may be considered the referent. Before elucidating Buzan's ideas it can easily be seen that, *for realists*, Buzan is opening a can of worms that may simply serve to obfuscate what they regard as the essential, timeless features of what constitutes security for *states* in the international system. Whilst criticism is easy, it is nonetheless the case that Buzan is broadening the security agenda so as to give it real relevance for the first time to a whole range of previously excluded actors and issues.

Amongst critics are Ken Booth, who argues that the book can 'primarily be read as an explanation of the difficulties surrounding the concept' of security and is rather unsatisfactory in that it fails to provide a new definition (1991, p. 317). Clearly, we disagree with the contention that a book on security must come up with a new definition to be useful! Implicit criticism of Buzan comes from Martin Shaw's persuasive argument for a critical sociological approach to understanding the concept of security. He suggests that 'the concept of social relations ... needs to be interposed between and around the terms "state" and "individual" within which the debate has been conducted' and that 'what is needed is a deepening as well as a broadening of the agenda', with the latter being seen as characteristic of Buzan's work (Shaw, 1993, p. 160). The argument that IR has been neglecting potentially useful insights from other disciplines is advanced more fully in the next chapter and particularly in Chapter 5.

Whilst from the perspective of today many of the criticisms offered of Buzan seem quite valid or even damning, we should not underestimate the 1983 volume's importance at least in a disciplinary context; whether this is in initiating the decline of security as the central organizing concept for IR or in helping prop up a doomed idea is debatable. However, Buzan and those of a like mind defend their approach even now (Buzan and Wæver, 1997). Buzan's work is most often criticized, because however welcome 'the recognition of additional dimensions of security [this] may be an *ad hoc* enlargement of a still state-centred concept of security' (Shaw, 1993, p. 162). Thus, despite a recognition of other referent objects existing when talking about security, it is nonetheless the case that Buzan emphasizes the importance, indeed the overriding importance, of state (and national) security; security is primarily about the fate of human collectivities and only secondarily about the personal security of individual human beings (1991a, p. 357).

Thus individuals are considered by Buzan to be of direct relevance in the study of security when 'in pursuing their own security, they may influence the higher levels of national or international security' (Shaw, 1993, p. 162). Buzan's conclusions, especially in the second edition of 1991, are actually more radical in appearance than the analysis presented in the preceding chapters. Thus, on the face of it, Buzan's work represents a bold, innovative step which will acknowledge the importance of many concerns relevant to third world peoples and society; he urges national security policy-makers to be far more aware of domestic implications and considerations. However, despite this superficial radicalism, Buzan's work is perhaps better seen as a catalyst to the thoughts of others – the tin-opener, beginning its task, for the can of worms with which this book deals. His work in widening the agenda brings in, or attracts, ideas from other social science disciplines to the study of security.

Clearly though, such a catalyst role is crucial and stems from a number of Buzan's ideas; incidentally, even he now seems happy to admit that his 'canon and indispensable reference point for students of security' (McSweeney, 1996, p. 81) 'was valuable because it helped to start a debate about the concept of security [but] was never intended to be the last word on the subject' (Buzan and Wæver, 1997, p. 250). It has also served as a springboard to help others, including its author, to formulate alternative positions.

Perhaps Buzan's most significant contribution is the recognition of the relationship between various actors in terms of security, particularly the ambiguity in terms of the relationship between states and individuals; 'for perhaps a majority of the world's people threats from the state are among the major sources of insecurity in their lives' (Buzan, 1991a, p. 45). Thus the state is not simply a provider of security but a source of insecurity.

Here Buzan breaks with other neorealists, such as Waltz (1959), in arguing that there are fundamental differences between different types of states with regard to security; namely that there are weak and strong ones, in which 'weak' does not signify individual freedom from threat and 'strong' does not signify threat from authoritarianism but rather the level of effectiveness with which each may provide a structure for the provision of security for its citizens. Hence with weak states, security can simply become a matter of the protection of a narrow elite group, or, in other words, regime security and the existence of a territory, if it is applied in the traditional realist manner (see Thomas and Saravanamuttu, 1987).[2]

These ideas of Buzan have been taken on and applied by third world scholars such as Mohammed Ayoob (1986) and Muthiah Alagappa (1987) to try to draw attention to the range of problems faced by the third world, whilst at the same time stressing the importance of state-building. Ayoob argues that the third world's 'security predicament' (see also Ayoob, 1995, 1997) is due, in part, to its collective stage in the state-building process. In a sense, this work acknowledges a range of threats faced by many poorer states (and people within them) but nonetheless suggests a very state-centric approach as fundamental to resolving problems or lessening threats. In such an analysis, the third world is still generalized, totalized and allocated a stage along the path to democracy and development reminiscent of Rostow's (1960) shallow 'stages of development' analysis, as much a political manifesto and parody as it is a convincing academic case (see Baran and Hobsbawm, 1973; also Chapters 1 and 6).

Ayoob's analysis, despite these shortcomings, does directly address the third world, though in an orthodox sense. He argues that the imposition of a Westphalian model in Asia, Africa and Latin America has been of little benefit to the indigenous peoples since problems are internal rather than external; the embracing of Westphalian values by local elites has seen a disjuncture between the security agendas of elites and the people. Thus Ayoob recognizes a whole range of insecurities throughout the third world but ultimately argues that it makes sense only to address these at the level of state-building.

Meanwhile, Alagappa's national security model addresses the issue of internal regime security more thoroughly than Buzan in that he recognizes the importance of focusing on levels below the state. Alagappa identifies three aspects that shape the internal security of weak or developing states: conflict over physical definition of the state; contending ideologies vying for power within the state; and lack of regime legitimacy. Alagappa therefore questions concepts of national security that assign threats predominantly to external sources and focus on the state as the referent object of national security. National security of third world states, he argues, must be related to the sub-state level (internal dimension). Only with such understanding of the importance of sub-state security can national security be linked with extra-regional or global security issues. State-to-state security relationships play a predominant role in precipitating conflict or facilitating security only when a dispute involves 'strong' states who enjoy broad-based legitimacy (Alagappa, 1987, p. 4). Like Ayoob, however, this framework retains the state as the primary unit of analysis, despite recognizing the importance of internal political legitimacy and political stability to national security. Whilst useful in the categorization, recognition and discussion of internal political and physical state conflict (insurgencies, factional disputes, irredentist movements and so on), his framework does not take into account other societal factors which are relevant.

Thus Buzan, Ayoob, Alagappa and others (Azar and Moon, 1988) tend to relegate the role of internal/individual security as being subordinate to the overall national security of the state, with Ayoob insisting that national security interests must be defined by the political realm in order to maintain the concept's utility as a conceptual tool; thus many internal threats and conflicts posed by human collectivities are not deemed *legitimate* threats to national security. Because of this, many problems relevant in a third world context – what we could call 'conditions of existence' – are only a problem for neorealist analyses when they threaten to spill over into a traditional realist security arena, thus becoming legitimate. For Ayoob, therefore, community, ecological or economic problems are only relevant to security when they 'threaten state boundaries, political institutions or governing regimes' (1995, p. 8).

We argue in subsequent chapters that these problems, in terms of the resistance they engender and coping strategies they give rise to, have more potential relevance in understanding and thinking about security than has been acknowledged by either realists or neorealists.

In effect then, some neorealists, of whom we have given a small sample here, have questioned who or what could qualify as the referent object of security but still within a framework where the state is the ultimate guarantor of not only military security but also other types of security. However, neorealism has also recognized different issues as relevant to a security agenda; this is an important step in taking security away from the exclusive control of strategic studies and giving it real relevance to a range of third world countries and areas within IR. The ideas of such neorealists can be said to be developing security as a conceptual tool (though seemingly truer of Buzan than Ayoob)[3] whilst remaining fundamentally state-centric.

Conclusions

Thus, rather than arguing that neorealists have made a fundamental difference in security studies with their ideas *per se*, it might be argued that these ideas have only minimally affected understandings of security. As we shall see, their relevance has been in terms of a catalyst effect, since neorealist analysis of security is still very much centred on the state. Despite this, the role of catalyst, whilst only speeding up a reaction rather than changing it, has clearly been important since the previous realist definition had allowed elites to disguise personal interest as national interest and had led to brutal and repressive policies in the name of national security.

Some would question even a catalyst role, arguing that 'International Relations in the 1990s remains fundamentally incarcerated in the positivistic-realist framework that characterized its understanding of the world "out there" in the 1940s and 1950s' (George, 1994, p. 14). It is to such criticisms, and to alternative ways of viewing what constitutes security, that we turn to more fully in the next chapter.

Consequently, another interpretation is that the role of Buzan and others has been, in effect, to prop up their preferred realist mode of analysis, prolonging its legitimacy and allowing it undue influence within the discipline in the light of contemporary critiques. Buzan's position is ambiguous; he opens his arms to the victims of realist (national) security policies, but he effectively shuts the door in their face before they reach him, so concerned is he to correct the invective against realism. It might well be argued, therefore, that the new legitimacy that Buzan gave to realist notions of security has held back IR, avoiding *any* revision of the basic theory (limiting rather than expanding political discourse), let alone encouraging the development, for instance, of normative micro-level security analyses with real relevance to third world peoples.

Just one example that work on security need not be state-centric has been convincingly stated by Martin Shaw (1993) in his argument for a more sociological approach to IR, with reference to the prominent sociologist Anthony Giddens. The latter's work 'provides a historical framework for analysing the changes in the nature of security between pre-modern and modern time' (Shaw, 1993, p. 173), a theme which is expounded by others using the concept of risk (Beck, 1992). However, despite a comprehensive treatment of security, Giddens hardly mentions the state at all, underlining the fact that informed debate about security is very much possible without doing so. This highlights the fact that whilst Buzan's was a highly novel approach *within* disciplinary IR, once other disciplinary influences were brought to bear upon both security and IR the radical appearance of Buzan's approach is soon exposed as a thin veneer (see Giddens, 1990).

Whether it was Buzan, in fact, who spurred on a whole new generation of security analysts to strive for deeper, more profound and subtle accounts of the concept, or whether he helped to hold back a tidal wave of epistemological, ontological and politico-ethical critiques is an issue which we shall, for the moment, leave to one side. The next chapter turns to examine possible new ways to explore security, and what it means to be secure in the context of the third world, in the form of postpositivist/poststructuralist critiques of IR. For the devotees of such positions, security would inevitably prove a target for sustained attack, though, as mentioned earlier, this process of criticism and counter-criticism has tended to be a two-way dialogue of the deaf. Following Jim George (1994, p. 3),

> in an emerging age of great dangers [that is, insecurities], complexities and opportunities in global life, it is crucial that we go beyond the simple ritualised representation of Traditional theory and practice and begin to seriously question that which for so long has evoked certain irreducible images of reality for the policy and intellectual communities in International Relations.

Finally, we might conclude that in opening security up in terms of issue areas as well as to previously neglected areas (the third world), the work of those such as Buzan, Ayoob and Alagappa has allowed the concept of security to broaden. In effect, what the rest of this book is concerned with is not simply asking how or why we might wish to attempt the broadening of security but with suggesting that we have at our disposal various ways of thinking which might encourage the deepening of the concept as well.

Notes

1. Reinhold Niebuhr and Martin Wight are often mentioned in this context, somewhat confusingly for being Christians – the point being of course that personal moral positions (Christian or otherwise) and feelings of despair *vis-à-vis* world politics do not conflict with faith in the scientific certainty of a realist position.
2. For a theoretical discussion and practical application of regime security and stability in the third world, see Alagappa (1987, 1988). For further discussion of aspects which shape the internal security of weak or developing states, see Alagappa (1987).
3. Such a view is based on looking at Buzan's 1983 edition of *People, States and Fear* and a later book of which he was one of the authors, *Identity, Migration and the New Security Agenda in Europe* (Wæver et al., 1993), and then comparing these with Ayoob's similarly spaced work (1986, 1995).

References

Alagappa, M. (1987) *The National Security of Developing States: Lessons from Thailand*. Dover: Auburn House.
Alagappa, M. (1988) 'Comprehensive security: interpretations in ASEAN countries'. In *Asian Security Issues: Regional and Global*, Berkeley, CA: Institute of East Asian Studies.
Aron, R. (1966) *Peace and War: A Theory of International Relations*. New York: Doubleday.
Ashley, R. (1984) 'The poverty of neo-realism', *International Organization*, 38 (2), 225–86.
Ayoob, M. (1986) *Regional Security Dilemmas in the Third World*. London: Croom Helm.
Ayoob, M. (1995) *The Third World Security Predicament*. Boulder, CO: Lynne Rienner.
Ayoob, M. (1997) 'Defining security: a subaltern realist perspective'. In Krause, K. and Williams, M. (eds) *Critical Security Studies*. London: UCL Press, pp. 121–46.
Azar, E. and Moon, M. (1988) *National Security in the Third World*. Aldershot: Edward Elgar.
Baran, P. and Hobsbawm, E. (1973) 'The stages of economic growth: a review'. In Wilber, C. (ed.) *The Political Economy of Development and Underdevelopment*, 1st edition. New York: Random House, pp. 45–54.

Bartleson, H. (1996) 'Short circuits: society and tradition in international relations theory', *Review of International Studies*, 22 (4), 339–60.
Beard, C.A. (1966) *The Idea of National Interest: An Analytical Study in American Foreign Policy*. Chicago: Quadrangle.
Beck, U. (1992) *Risk Society*. London: Sage.
Berridge, G. (1992) *International Politics*, 2nd edition. London: Harvester Wheatsheaf.
Booth, K. (1991) 'Security and emancipation', *Review of International Studies*, 17 (3), 313–26.
Bull, H. (1977) *The Anarchical Society: A Study of Order in World Politics*. Basingstoke: Macmillan.
Burchill, S. and Linklater, A. (1996) *Theories of International Relations*. London: Macmillan.
Buzan, B. (1983) *People, States and Fear: The National Security Problem in International Relations*, 1st edition. Brighton: Wheatsheaf.
Buzan, B. (1989) 'The concept of security for developing states'. In Ayoob, M. and Samudavanija, C.-A. (eds) *Leadership Perceptions and National Security: The Southeast Asian Experience*. Singapore: Institute of Southeast Asian Studies.
Buzan, B. (1991a) *People, States and Fear: An Agenda for International Security Studies in the Post Cold War Era*, 2nd edition. Hemel Hempstead: Harvester Wheatsheaf.
Buzan, B. (1991b) 'New patterns of global security in the 21st century', *International Affairs*, 67 (3), 431–52.
Buzan, B. (1992) 'Third world regional security in structural and historical perspective'. In Job, B. (ed.) (1992) *The Insecurity Dilemma*. Boulder, CO: Lynne Rienner.
Buzan, B. and Wæver, O. (1997) 'Slippery? Contradictory? Sociologically untenable? The Copenhagen school replies', *Review of International Studies*, 23 (2), 241–50.
Campbell, D. (1992) *Writing Security*. Manchester: Manchester University Press.
Carr, E.H. (1964) *The Twenty Years Crisis, 1919–1939: An Introduction to the Study of International Relations*, 3rd edition. New York: Harper and Row.
Deudney, D. (1991) 'The case against linking environmental degradation and national security', *Millennium*, 19 (3), 461–76.
George, J. (1994) *Discourses of Global Politics: A Critical (Re)Introduction to International Relations*. London: Macmillan.
Giddens, A. (1990) *The Consequences of Modernity*. Cambridge: Cambridge University Press.
Giddens, A. (1991) *Modernity and Self-Identity: Self and Society in the Late Modern Age*. Cambridge: Polity Press.
Herz, J. (1950) 'Idealist internationalism and the security dilemma', *World Politics*, (2).
Jervis, R. (1976) *Perception and Misperception in International Politics*. Princeton: Princeton University Press.
Jervis, R. (1991) 'The spiral of international security'. In Smith, M. and Little, R. (eds) *Perspectives in World Politics*. London: Routledge, pp. 91–101.
McSweeney, B. (1996) 'Identity and security: Buzan and the Copenhagen school', *Review of International Studies*, 22 (1), 81–94.
Morgenthau, H. J. (1978) *Politics among Nations: The Struggle for Power and Peace*, 5th edition. New York: Alfred Knopf.
Niebuhr, R. (1953) *Christian Realism and Political Problems*. New York: Charles Scribner's Sons.

Pettiford, L. and Poku, N. (1996) *Understanding International Relations*. Nottingham: Pokular Press.

Rostow, W.W. (1960) *Stages of Economic Growth*. Cambridge: Cambridge University Press.

Shaw, M. (1993) ' "There is no such thing as society": beyond individualism and statism in international security studies', *Review of International Studies*, 19 (2), 159–76.

Smith, M.J. (1986) *Realist Thought: From Weber to Kissinger*. Baton Rouge, LA: University of Louisiana Press.

Thomas C. and Saravanamutta, P. (1987) *In Search of Security: The Third World in International Relations*. Brighton: Wheatsheaf.

Thucydides (1998) *The Peloponnesian War* (a new translation by W. Blanco, edited by W. Blanco and J. Tolbert Roberts). New York: Norton.

Tickner, J.A. (1995) 'Re-visioning security'. In Booth, K. and Smith, S. (eds) *International Relations Theory Today*. Cambridge: Polity Press, pp. 175–97.

Vasquez, J. (1983) *The Power of Power Politics*, London: Pinter.

Wæver, O. et al. (1993) *Identity, Migration and the New Security Agenda in Europe*. London: Pinter.

Walt, S. (1991) 'The renaissance of security studies', *International Studies Quarterly*, 35 (2), 211–37.

Waltz, K. (1959) *Man, the State and War*. New York: Columbia University Press.

Waltz, K. (1979) *Theory of International Politics*. New York: McGraw Hill.

Wendt, A. (1991) 'Bridging the theory/meta-theory gap in international relations', *Review of International Studies*, 17 (4), 383–92.

Wight, M. (1978) *Power Politics*. Leicester: Leicester University Press.

Wolfers, A. (1963) *Britain and France between the Two Wars: Conflicting Strategies of Peace since Versailles*. Hamden, CT: Archon.

3

Critical Theory and Postmodernism: The Challenges[1]

Just as Buzan (1983) was giving serious consideration to the central organizing concept of International Relations (IR), that of security, within the mainstream realist/neorealist school, IR was itself finally subjected to radical critique by the 1980s; perhaps more accurately the 'backward discipline' was increasingly unable to justify this situation and finally felt the effects of trends which had affected other areas of the social sciences sometimes decades before (George, 1994). To questions of the *purpose* of the discipline (first raised before and after the Second World War), *methodology* (subject of the so-called second great debate of the 1960s) and, to a lesser extent, of *ontological choice* (raised in the 1970s in the form of discussion of the relevance of transnational actors and so on) were added *epistemological* questions (that is, questions concerning how we make claims about knowledge, how we know what we know) and *ethical* questions (once more enquiry into what the purpose and moral basis of IR's intellectual endeavour should be). In this sense, 'fortress IR' was simply catching up with other areas of the social sciences. As George argues in this context, some very important questions 'can no longer be ignored by scholars engaged, perhaps more than any others, with everyday questions of life and death' (1994, p. 33).

Thus, for some within IR (who together are often subsumed under the label poststructuralism or postmodernism), it is not clear whether Buzan's work on security can serve as anything more than a series of '*caveats* to a state-centred notion of security; complex qualifications which in the end preserve the integrity of the [realist] project more or less intact' (Shaw, 1993, p. 163). For such people 'far from reinforcing traditional international relations concepts, it is necessary to subject them to sustained criticism' (p. 159). Others have been quite kind in their criticisms, at least in footnotes; but for critical social theorists the realist concern that Buzan's work is opening a can of worms is exactly its strength, perhaps its only strength, rather than the intrinsic value of its ideas. For this reason, George argues that whilst he does not want to 'trivialise Buzan's contribution' since 'there is much to applaud in his thoughtful approach' Buzan's work nonetheless 'remains an example of "repressed" modernist critique' (1994, p. 218). Put simply, critical and postmodern theorists, whose arguments form the basis of this chapter, would argue that the worms had been canned for far too long anyway and needed to be untangled and deconstructed in all their complexity rather than ignored.

Of course such contributions have not passed without a reactionary backlash. Stephen Walt, for instance, suggests security studies 'should remain wary of the counter-productive tangents that have seduced other areas of international relations, most notably the "post-modern" approach to international affairs' (1991, p. 223). However, just as Jim George's admonishing of realism for being an over-simplification (see Chapter 2) is unlikely to worry realists, so the anger in Walt's contention that postmodernism is a 'self-indulgent discourse that is divorced from the real world' is unlikely to hit the mark (1991, p. 223); just as realists regard their (over)simplification as a strength rather than weakness (the necessary distilled essence to aid understanding), postmodernism is concerned to stress the impossibility of unicausality and an actually existing single *real* world that we can look to for evidence to test our hypotheses objectively. Whilst these ideas are explained and expanded upon below, here it is worth noting that in emphasizing diversity rather than uniformity, in eschewing the notion of law-like generalities, we can see how such a perspective is likely to (a) bring the third world in and (b) recognize 'third world' not as a category but almost as a shifting debate with multiple meanings existing simultaneously.

Critical theory and postmodernism often get put in the same chapter or follow each other in successive chapters because of their role in raising the epistemological questions which are alluded to above and discussed below. Both approaches share a similar role, in provoking a situation where the '(t)radition and discipline of International Relations, framed in modernist terms and articulated primarily within positivist-Realist principles of understanding, have been re-written, respoken and reconceptualised in recent years' (George, 1994, p. 171). Despite this common role, as part of a disciplinary *poststructuralist* turn in the late 1980s, it should not be forgotten that critical theory and postmodernism are very different, with different theoretical antecedents from diverse areas within critical social theory; broadly speaking, whilst critical theory offers a radical reorientation of the Enlightenment project itself,[2] postmodernism is a critique and rejection of it.[3] What they do share is a poststructuralist epistemology and a recent emergence in IR and hence their frequent treatment as one. Furthermore, the level of criticism that each has for the other tends to be notably less than the invective reserved for realism (see Hansen, 1997).

The linkages of both critical theory and postmodernism to much feminist theory is noticeable (see Steans, 1998) and all three have, in recent years, had ever greater influence in IR. Feminism, in the sense that it is 'considered a topical sub-field of IR', has achieved 'the partial inclusion, rather than the serious integration of feminist perspectives in IR' (True, 1996, p. 212) and, along with postmodernism, can more properly be defined as a critique of the discipline. Furthermore, on many IR courses feminist perspectives are not taught coherently (and are taught by male-dominated departments) and tend to be included in a somewhat tokenistic manner.

The primary aim of this chapter then is to outline ways in which these increasingly influential tools might be used when thinking about security and the third world. Critical theory will be considered first, but in doing so we note in this section the sometimes wider, almost ambiguous offshoot known as critical security studies. At times critical security studies has seemed to be a broader church than simply a critical theoretical approach to security – more a framework incorporating virtually any revision of the realist concept including those such as Buzan and those who have taken their inspiration from him. As we have already suggested, there is a strong case for arguing that Buzan's apparently catalytic approach did in fact tie up IR in a type of debate which was far from critical, in a way that will be elucidated below, and which left certain epistemological assumptions unchallenged and intact. We are more concerned to discuss critical theoretical approaches and how they might help us to think about security.

The chapter then deals with postmodernism. In the context of traditional (mainstream/malestream) IR, this is most often a critique. It is not concerned with setting a solid agenda, nor with science-like laws, but with pointing to the biases and investments of those who do. Thus postmodernists engage, for instance, in a deconstruction of IR's foundational texts or genealogical analysis of some of its key terms. As Campbell aptly puts it, the aim 'has not been to dismiss the dominant readings, but to illustrate that they are, indeed, *readings*' (George, 1994, p. 192); that is, to demonstrate that they are, in fact, no more than spatio-temporally specific *accounts* – a version *of* truth rather than *the* truth. This has particular interest to us in the context of exactly what is 'securitized'. Put another way, who defines a security issue and how they define it is a crucial question to ponder.

Finally, the chapter will consider feminism (frequently tied in with the post-positivist literature) and look at the notion of gendered insecurity. Whilst much of the feminist literature in IR comes from a critical or postmodern vein, here we sketch its particular features. In the context of a (third) world in which the 'feminization of poverty' is an increasing trend we believe that feminist perspectives on security provide an interesting avenue for study (see Steans, 1998, Chapter 5).

In the sense that both critical theory and postmodernism (and much feminist scholarship) question the underlying bases of the notion of an independently existing 'reality' which is 'out there' and subject to timeless laws, these approaches are important if security is to become relevant in third world contexts. In the words of one postmodern scholar, the third world is increasingly characterized by 'conflict between elites seeking to control (in one way or another) the consequences of the internationalisation of production upon their societies and the (often) disenfranchised masses seeking (in one way or another) to confront the everyday misery of their existence' (George, 1994, p. 196). Accordingly, the status quo orientation of mainstream theory, and its relationship to practice stand in the way of a vast number of people attempting to change this existence of misery, that is, attaining even a minimal sense of what could be termed security. Both critical theory and postmodernism provide useful ways to think about this book's main concerns. Both stand firmly against universalizing and totalizing notions of realist security and meta-narratives as a basis for theoretical and ethical understanding(s) of international relations. This helps in undermining, for instance, simplistic developmentalist prescriptions for the 'third world'. These are based on the advice of foreign experts as a means for providing 'basic needs' which seem to reduce security to mere existence.[4] 'Our age is one whose horizon is described by global considerations and dangers of *unique kinds and proportions* [emphasis added]. Dangers which are a function of our forms of life' (Campbell and Dillon, 1993, p. 4). In this context, the tools outlined below may be very useful in helping to think about security in terms of 'life chances' rather than as a measurable aspect of external reality.

Critical Theory

Critical theory, despite various antecedents, is most closely associated with a body of thought known as the Frankfurt school, a fairly diverse body of work including that of Adorno, Horkheimer, Marcuse and Habermas among others. In broader historical context, as Devetak observes, critical theory's 'normative interest in identifying immanent possibilities for social transformation is a defining characteristic of a line of thought which extends, at least, from Kant, through Marx, to contemporary critical theorists such as Habermas' (1996, p. 147). In considering a way of interpreting security which might have direct relevance to the third world, we are drawn immediately to the words 'normative interest' and 'social transformation'. Following on from the previous chapter, we should note that 'whereas neorealism [has] helped to legitimate an order which the powerful found congenial, critical theory [has] looked for immanent possibilities that it might be transformed to satisfy the interests of the marginal and excluded' (Linklater, 1990, p. 256). Part of the 'critical' project of critical theory is to ask not how the world has come to be this way, but how the world can be *other than* it is.

It seems important to stress, however, that the Frankfurt school has barely bothered itself with addressing international relations, and that critical theory came to fore in the 1960s and 1970s as an intellectual attack on traditional forms of sociology. In today's IR, various scholars such as Andrew Linklater, Robert Cox, Mark Hoffman and others are associated with 'critical *international* theory [which] takes the global configuration of power relations as its object and asks how that configuration came about, what costs it brings with it, and what other possibilities remain immanent in history' (Devetak, 1996, p. 151). Such a focus clearly questions the close link between power and security in conventional understandings of international relations and the relevance that this might have in the context of the current study should be apparent from the outset; for critical theorists 'the impact of internationalisation of production upon peripheral state structures is as important... as conflict between states is to realism' (Linklater, 1990, p. 30).

In the context of security, critical international theory has been particularly concerned by the status quo orientation of realism and the fact that the 'focus is on the means with which to achieve a given end rather than the validity of the end itself' (Devetak, 1996, p. 152). Realism is criticized for its (state-based/military) uni-dimensionality but, at a deeper level, 'of advocating a political practice which [has] stifled the forces which revealed that new patterns of historical development might be possible' (Linklater, 1990, p. 3). Since realism does not allow for the possibility of change it provides no philosophical basis for a reconceptualization of security. In effect, realism's theoretical agenda maintains security's conceptual clarity and this same clarity sets the policy agenda in international relations. If we privilege the state ontologically as a pre-eminent entity and as the only deserving referent of security in international relations, we in effect support a hegemony, in the Gramscian sense, that precludes analysis of the insecurity experienced by individuals, groups and communities at the sub-state level; thus critical theory is interested in the existence and possibility of counter-hegemonic forces, how these mediate dominant security and development discourses and hence contribute to different understandings of security and of what should be securitized. Such a stance is crucial in alleviating the implicit despair of realism where 'rational behaviour in the context of anarchy *inevitably reproduces* [emphasis added] the very condition of distrust and insecurity which threatens all states' (Linklater, 1990, p. 12).

Thus for critical theorists, security is understood first and foremost as being about the absence of threat. It is linked with notions of a universal emancipation and autonomy leading to freedom of action and hence real, or true, security. Critical security studies is therefore reacting against the problem-solving of traditional security studies, preferring to challenge the hegemonic security discourse and prevailing practices of global (in)-security. Problem-solving theory is that which accepts the prevailing order, its socio-political relations and institutions and seeks to 'make these relationships and institutions work smoothly by dealing effectively with particular sources of trouble' (Linklater, 1990, pp. 27–8). In asking how the prevailing order and its relevant institutions came about, critical theory in effect questions the very framework that problem-solving theory takes as its starting-point. In the context of security, the questions which are fundamentally asked are definitional as well as concerning what is actually secure in the prevailing order. With whose security should we really be concerned? Who or what needs to be secured?

In the context of IR and critical theory we should not forget the influence of Antonio Gramsci's anti-structuralist Marxism. As with the Frankfurt school, Gramsci was not concerned to write at length upon international relations (and even less so on its disciplinary form) but, as someone concerned with promoting revolution in the advanced capitalist countries, his ideas on the state have nonetheless had significant recent influence in IR. For Gramsci, the state is 'the entire complex of practical and theoretical activities with which the ruling class not only justifies and maintains its dominance but manages to win the active consent of those over whom it rules' (Jessop, 1982, p. 147). From this we can see that emancipation is not simply about the forceful overthrow of the physical apparatus of the state, and that emancipatory politics signifies more than a move from capitalism to socialism. Along with Walker we are thus inclined to agree upon the importance of critical social movements and on 'their capacity to alter our understanding of what power can be' (Walker, 1988, p. 146).

Critical theory and its generalized concern with the human predicament have made some serious converts among the established IR community; the most notable example is perhaps Ken Booth, who began to question the core assumptions of mainstream security discourse within a critical security/emancipation framework. The extent to which Booth says anything particularly novel is somewhat debatable; however, his work *has* achieved significant attention. His Carr-like ideas do at least provide an important counterpoint to Buzan's neorealism, as well as his own earlier work. The above is not intended to represent a personal attack and Booth's malestream endeavours were/are more subtle than many; the conversion is but an example of the increasing relevance of critical approaches in IR and the declining attractiveness of realism (see Carr, 1964; Booth, 1990, 1991a, 1991b).

To sum up then, critical theory is about challenging the natural, the 'unchallengeable', and it is about human emancipation. In challenging a realist orthodoxy whose core assumptions privilege states, and powerful states at that, critical theory opens the way for analysis not only of poorer states but also of peoples whose lives have been characterized by poverty. The *concerns* of postmodernism have not always been so very different; what follows should help to adumbrate the differences of approach in a clear fashion, particularly regarding the status of the Enlightenment project.

Postmodernism

There seems to be a tendency amongst many students (and indeed lecturers) of IR to shy away from postmodernism.[5] In a discipline which remained firmly entrenched for so long in realist dogma this is hardly surprising, and students who frequently begin courses by learning the simple realist essence are often reluctant to let go. Some students seem to feel that whilst realism's conservatism goes against their personal morality, it might be better for them to remain realists because it is simple to understand! This is understandable. When something seeks to undermine centuries of thinking within particular confines then it is hardly likely to be obvious to a mind brought up within those confines. The situation is further complicated by the need to learn a new vocabulary to join in with postmodernists; however, this may be true of playing squash, eating in Indian restaurants and myriad other things in life and should not put one off. For those familiar with this vocabulary, however, the following may sound unnecessarily simplified. The 'for' or 'against' nature of postmodernism's involvement in IR may well lead to one or other perception for students.

This section seeks to outline postmodernism and the claims it makes in more detail, and to assess the possible implications for security studies. Ultimately, we believe that postmodernism provides a highly satisfying perspective for those who would view world politics 'from the vantage point of the marginalized, silenced, the omitted [and] those whose lives, cultures, and histories have, for so long, been read out of the power politics narrative' (George, 1994, pp. 211–12). For our purposes, therefore, it seems a promising avenue of enquiry in terms of thinking about security in a third world context.

In general, postmodernists demand, at the very minimum, a serious renegotiation of modernity; in the context of this book, they 'have sought to reconceptualize the strategic/security discourse by opening it to questions that its traditional agenda continues to ignore or marginalise' (George, 1994, p. 209). The modern stage of human existence (modernity) we can outline as associated with modern scientific methods, individualism and state sovereignty replacing that of the church. Thus postmodernists take issue with the contemporary philosophical, scientific and moral derivatives of the products of the Enlightenment period of history. Ideas of progress from the Enlightenment are an important presence in the idea of 'modernity'. Teodor Shanin, for example, argues that barring a few temporary deviations 'all societies are advancing naturally and consistently "up", on a route from poverty, barbarism, despotism and ignorances to riches, civilization, democracy and rationality, the highest expression of which is science'. Interestingly for realist theory, he notes the 'most significant material representation and instrument of the idea of progress has been the modern state, with its legitimation as the representation of the nation, its claims to bureaucratic rationality and... its strategies resting on a notion of progress linked to the power to disburse privileges and to enforce ways and means'. Rather than see the struggle for power within states as primary, Shanin argues they were 'usually disguised as debate about the interpretation of the objective laws of progress' (Shanin, 1997, p. 69).

Whilst modernism is associated with science and certainty (perhaps including prescriptions offered by critical theorists), postmodernists 'offer indeterminacy rather than determinism, diversity rather than unity, difference rather than synthesis, complexity rather than simplification. [They] look to the unique rather than to the general, to intertextual relations rather than causality, and to the unrepeatable rather than the reoccurring, the habitual or routine' (Rosenau, 1992, p. 8). With such an approach it is hardly surprising that the idea of truth (and the foundational truths of realism) is seen very differently from the way it is within the positivistic social sciences, including traditional IR.

Postmodernism as a critique of mainstream IR seeks to subvert its positivistic methodological, ontological and epistemological presumptions; it rejects ideas such as rationality, logic, objective truth and reason, in effect being anti-foundationalist. Postmodernism critiques positivistic theory as being simply truth claims serving to justify the interests of the powerful; this strikes at the very core of realist security. For postmodernists such as Foucault, truth and ideology are very similar, with ideology as a truth claim of the powerful; 'we are subjected to the reproduction of truth through power, and we cannot exercise power except through the production of truth' (Foucault, 1980, p. 132). For Foucault, the relationship between power and knowledge is central to the discussion around truth. Foucault's project to consider the relationship between power, knowledge and truth could be summarized as an analysis of discourse to discover how *knowledge* comes to function within society; an analysis of *power* to discover how power defines truth within discourse to define 'knowledge'; and an analysis of how power functions to make humans *subject* to this 'knowledge'.

For Foucault, a discourse could be defined as 'a system of possibility of knowledge' where a body of rules define and restrict the statements individuals make; collectively these statements constitute 'truths' which are autonomous within that discourse (Phelen, 1990, p. 422). What is considered to be knowledge functions within discourse as accepted truth. In this sense, accepted truth is knowledge. Put another way, discourse is a 'matrix of social practices that gives meaning to the way that people understand themselves and their behaviour [thus] generat[ing] the categories of meaning by which reality can be understood and explained'. Put simply in this context, realism makes *real* that which it prescribes as *meaningful* (George, 1994, pp. 29–30). Therefore issues such as gender and ecology are not part of realism as a discursive formation.

Thus realist IR's claim to capture the essence of security and international relations, that is *the* essential truth, based on a number of claims about the nature of the individual, the state and the international system (and the natural timeless aspect of the whole thing), is no more than a historically specific justification of the powerful and currently existing power relations. Clearly, if we talk about security in the sense of being secure, then only the most powerful, be it countries or individuals, can make any claim to having attained security.

Postmodernism has become at once fashionable, misunderstood and ridiculed within the social sciences, in particular IR, and its transplantation from literary studies has not been easy, resulting in significant confusion and dissatisfaction. This is not least to do with the alien vocabulary alluded to in the opening paragraph of this section. For those who are at least dubious about the merits of sceptical postmodernism (that is, postmodernism at its most uncompromising), it is difficult not to become irritated by what may appear pretensions and to conclude that postmodernism really is an invention of academics to help justify and maintain their positions! At its most radical it might be said that postmodernism becomes impenetrable nihilistic nonsense. It has undoubtedly developed from a sense of meaninglessness which can be associated with modern life. In defence of postmodernism at a level of intellectual importance greater than simply dissatisfaction with modern life, we should note that postmodernism has been used most effectively to raise questions regarding those who are marginalized or silenced by dominant *discourses* and to highlight the inadequacies of 'scientific' social science (Rosenau, 1992, p. 10).

Postmodernism's 'anti-meta-narrative meta-narrative', as it has been somewhat sarcastically dubbed,[6] thus provides a damning critique of realism's grand theory and, in terms of security and the texts associated with it, makes us aware of what is not said (of the marginalized voices and the oppressed of this world) as well as a very selective reading of the discipline's foundational texts; for example, within realism it can be argued that 'Machiavelli has been reduced to a figure of parody and caricature by those seeking philosophical certainty for their image of the contemporary world of states' and much the same can be said of the work of Thucydides (George, 1994, p. 194).[7] By its very nature, postmodernism does not represent a united theory of any kind but makes us aware of the danger of accepting the claims of those who do. In sensitizing us to difference and the dangers of universalizing, essentializing, totalizing theory, postmodernism has great significance, not for the third world as a geographically bounded notion of the past, but for the security, in a multifaceted sense, of peoples throughout the globe who are in some sense marginalized from the first world, where 'first world' is understood as a world of privilege and power.

Postmodernism has introduced methods of analysis and research to help make visible power relations which have previously silenced marginalized voices. Through adopting discourse analysis and other Foucauldian methods, Escobar (1995), for example, tries to show how the 'third world' emerged as a category from the postwar discourse of development which utilized powerful mechanisms of control and intervention in third world countries (see also Chapter 6).

Before moving on to feminism it is worth 'making real' some of the foregoing by looking briefly at part of James Der Derian's genealogy of security in Campbell and Dillon's 1993 edited collection, *The Political Subject of Violence*. Like all genealogies, Der Derian's is designed 'to stimulate our appreciation of the discursive power of the concept, to remember its forgotten meanings [and] to assess its economy of use in the present' (Campbell and Dillon, 1993, p. 29). Der Derian begins by asking just how secure is the pre-eminent concept of IR; by now this should be apparent, but it is nonetheless the case that 'no other concept in international relations[8] packs the metaphysical punch, nor commands the disciplinary power of "security"'. In looking at Stephen Walts' essay entitled 'The renaissance of security studies', Der Derian suggests that 'one is left with the suspicion that the rapid changes in world politics have triggered a "security crisis" in security studies that requires extensive theoretical damage control' (1993, pp. 94–6). In this sense we might see some of the post-Buzan work as damage limitation in the face of epistemological attacks on traditional IR rather than a genuinely open debate.

Der Derian argues that crucial epistemological, ontological and political questions are 'all too often ignored, subordinated, or displaced by the technically biased, narrowly framed question of *what* it takes to achieve security'. This basically supports the criticism of strategic studies which we offered earlier. In adopting such an approach 'weapons of mass destruction have been developed which transfigured national interest into a security dilemma based on a suicide pact'. Der Derian goes on to suggest that 'the hope is that in the interpretation of the most pressing dangers of late modernity we might be able to construct a form of security based on the appreciation and articulation rather than the normalisation or extirpation of differences' and that 'if security is to have any significance for the future, it must find a home in the new disorder by a commensurate deterritorialisation of theory'. Here we would suggest parallels with a less geographically deterministic appreciation of the third world.

The foregoing is only intended as a flavour of the arguments presented. Der Derian goes on to examine different historical usages of the word security (at least three), as well as the work of Marx and Nietzsche and Baudrillard's work on the *simulation syndrome*. The point of the analysis, however, is to support the contention that 'the unproblematical essence that is often attached to the term today does not stand up to even a cursory investigation' (Der Derian, 1993, pp. 97–109).

Feminism

> Feminists, together with non-feminist critical and postmodern IR scholars, claim that we can learn much about world politics by paying attention to the discipline's empirical, theoretical and political exclusions which make possible and give meaning to those agents, characteristics and outcomes that are ostensibly included in IR. (True, 1996, p. 211)

This sentiment reinforces the fundamental reasons behind the inclusion of feminism in this chapter; at the same time, it must be remembered that feminism (or feminisms) does not merely represent a contemporary development in the sociology of knowledge but 'is embedded in a rich and varied history of women's struggle and women theorising from the experience of struggle' (*ibid*.). The term 'feminisms' is used here because although we are attempting to relate feminism to two particular ideas or concepts, namely security and the third world, there is in fact a rich variety within feminist thought. There are, for example, conservative, liberal, Marxist, eco-, radical and psychoanalytical feminisms, amongst others.

Relating feminism empirically to a broadened critical security agenda, the statistics strongly indicate that insecurity (or lack of life chances) is gendered, with this lack of security frequently compounding other sources of insecurity such as race, poverty and rural dwelling. A man who is born in the Bolivian countryside to a poor Indian family may have little chance of ever rising above the poverty line; however, a woman born in similar circumstances has virtually no chance at all. In similar empirical fashion, the 'impact on' approach has shown how women suffer most as a result of militarism, in terms both of direct military spending and of the inherently violent societies which are created. The feminization of poverty is a frequently used phrase in the context of empirical analyses of women's struggle. Most feminists would agree that an 'impact on' approach may be a necessary, but not sufficient, basis for feminist analysis. It is certainly a 'way into' thinking about gender and security.

In the example given above neither man nor woman has much chance of achieving what might be called in critical security studies, true security (Booth, 1991a). Some have argued, however, that feminists engage with the oppression of all people regardless of gender (see Grant, 1992). In this sense feminism has at times become a discourse of the oppressed where the individual is the prime referent of security. Thus for Tickner the goal of a feminist security discourse would be not simply to address the insecurities felt by women but 'to point out how unequal social relations can make all individuals insecure' and to 'help conceptualize a definition of security that is people centred and transcends state and regional boundaries' (Tickner, 1995, pp. 193–4). On the other hand, with the gender aspect frequently ignored, some argue that addressing gender might easily be the key to ending the general oppression. However, feminists have not simply provided a new way of expressing, such as socialist ideas, but a concern with what is *omitted* from our understanding of security when gender is ignored.

Some feminists, in postmodern fashion, have sought to expose the masculinist myths and biases in foundational texts and concepts of IR such as found in the classical realism of Machiavelli and Hobbes. Based on such texts, feminists seek to show how women have, in effect, become invisible in the discipline due to the naturalization of profound gender bias. Within realist conceptions of security, the concept is tied to a nationalist political identity which is constructed using exclusionary practices which depend on the existence of an 'other'. Campbell (1992) suggests that threats to security in conventional thinking are all in the external realm and that the state requires this discourse of danger to secure its identity and legitimation. Feminists have contributed greatly to our understanding of processes of exclusion involved in the construction of the dangerous and threatening 'other' by showing how it is intimately connected with the construction of masculinity and the denial of the feminized other.

Feminism not only has sought to make IR gender sensitive but also has brought a global perspective to the study of women, highlighting multiple differentiations inherent in global structures and processes. In this latter context, as feminists have sought to highlight multiple oppressions, they are unravelling a whole series of security concerns. Since oppression and threat (one source of insecurity) can be considered so closely linked, this is not at all surprising. As feminists in IR have been concerned not simply with gender but also with hierarchies of race and class, we can immediately see their contributions' relevance in terms of a radically reorientated concept of security.

Conclusions

Comparing the perspectives highlighted above and the previous chapter on neorealism, one can see why IR was branded the backward discipline; its focus has been narrow and its blindness to developments in critical social theory regrettable. In terms of security realism has been obsessed with state security, and neorealism might be objected to on the grounds that it has provided a smokescreen for the continued domination of such a view. Within this theoretical view, political practice in the real world often saw (and sees) national security policies resulting in torture and misery for individuals and sub-state communities, whilst benefiting state elites.

We might object to the above on moral/normative grounds, and indeed many of the writers associated with the approaches dealt with in this chapter have done so. However, neorealism also neglects, or deals inadequately with, crucial contemporary issues such as the environment. Accordingly, we might further object that a state focus ultimately threatens the very states on which it gazes. The critical approaches outlined in this chapter give hope for an alternative future and for a more serious engagement with the marginalized – the third world.

Notes

1. The challenge of this chapter is to encapsulate what is important about these challenges whilst making them useful and comprehensible to students. This will inevitably fail to satisfy some at the cutting edge of theoretical debate, but the wrath of such people is considered a small price to pay for the demystifying of certain ideas.
2. See Chapter 5 for a discussion of Bacon and Descartes in the context of shifting attitudes to nature.

3. Both the tensions and the sympathies between critical theory and postmodernism are well demonstrated by Chapters 7 and 8 of George's *Discourses of Global Politics* (1994).
4. The relationship, or non-relationship, between statist IR's notion of security and the Development Studies literature, as well as a consideration of micro-level security analyses possibly developing from this relationship, is examined more closely in Chapter 6.
5. The discipline seems characterized by a fundamental split between those who embrace such ideas and those who reject them out of hand.
6. By our friend Dr Adam Cobb.
7. George also notes that 'it is worth recalling Isaiah Berlin's proposition that there are at least twenty-eight major interpretations of Machiavelli's textual legacy acknowledged by political theorists. [However,] International Relations continues to insist on only one – the power politics interpretation, which... is little more than a crude and opportunistic caricature of a complex and sophisticated body of work' (p. 227).
8. As with Campbell earlier, Der Derian is using lower case where the convention of this book would suggest the use of upper case.

References

Booth, K. (1990) *New Thinking about Strategy and International Security*. London: Unwin Hyman.

Booth, K. (1991a) 'Security and emancipation', *Review of International Studies*, 17 (3), 313–26.

Booth, K. (1991b) 'Security in anarchy: utopian realism in theory and practice', *International Affairs*, 67 (3), 527–45.

Buzan, B. (1983) *People, States and Fear: The National Security Problem in International Relations*, 1st edition. Brighton: Harvester.

Campbell, D. (1992) *Writing Security: United States Foreign Policy and the Politics of Identity*. Manchester: Manchester University Press.

Campbell, D. and Dillon, M. (eds) (1993) *The Political Subject of Violence*. Manchester: Manchester University Press.

Carr, E.H. (1964) *The Twenty Years Crisis, 1919–1939: An Introduction to the Study of International Relations*, 3rd edition. New York: Harper and Row.

Der Derian, J. (1993) 'The value of security: Hobbes, Marx, Nietzsche and Baudrillard'. In Campbell, D. and Dillon, M. (eds) *The Political Subject of Violence*. Manchester: Manchester University Press, pp. 94–109.

Devetak, R. (1996) 'Critical theory'. In Burchill, S. and Linklater, A. *Theories of International Relations*. London: Macmillan, pp. 179–209.

Escobar, A. (1995) *Encountering Development: The Making and Unmaking of the Third World*. Princeton: Princeton University Press.

Foucault, M. (1980) *Power/Knowledge: Selected Interviews and Other Writings, 1972–1977*. London: Harvester Wheatsheaf.

George, J. (1994) *Discourses of Global Politics: A Critical (Re)Introduction to International Relations*. London: Macmillan.

Giddens, A. (1990) *Modernity and Self-Identity: Self and Society in the Late Modern Age*. Cambridge: Polity Press.

Gill, S. (ed.) (1993) *Gramsci, Historical Materialism and International Relations*. Cambridge: Cambridge University Press.

Grant, R. (1992) 'The quagmire of gender and international security'. In Peterson, V.S. (ed.) *Gendered States: Feminist (Re)Visions of International Relations*. Boulder, CO: Lynne Rienner.

Hansen, L. (1997) 'A case for seduction? Evaluating the poststructuralist conceptualization of security', *Conflict and Cooperation*, 32 (4), 369–98.

Hoffman, M. (1987) 'Critical theory and the inter-paradigm debate', *Millennium*, 16 (2), 231–49.

Jessop, B. (1982) *The Capitalist State: Marxist Theories and Methods*. New York: New York University Press.

Jessop, B. (1990) *State Theory: Studies in and beyond Capitalist States*. Cambridge: Polity Press.

Keohane, R. (ed.) (1990) *Neo-Realism and Its Critics*. New York: Columbia University Press.

Linklater, A. (1990) *Beyond Realism and Marxism: Critical Theory and International Relations*. London: Macmillan.

Phelen, S. (1990) 'Foucault and feminism', *American Journal of Political Science*, 34 (2), 421–40.

Rahnema, M. (1991) 'Global poverty: a pauperising myth', *Interculture*, 24 (2), 4–51.

Rosenau, P. (1992) *Postmodernism and the Social Sciences: Insights, Inroads and Intrusions*. Princeton: Princeton University Press.

Shanin, T. (1997) 'The idea of progress'. In Rahnema, M. (ed.) *The Post-Development Reader*. London: Zed Books, pp. 65–72.

Shaw, M. (1993) ' "There is no such thing as society": beyond individualism and statism in international security studies', *Review of International Studies*, 19 (2), 159–76.

Steans, J. (1998) *Gender and International Relations: An Introduction*. London: Polity Press.

Tickner, J.A. (1995) 'Re-visioning security'. In Booth, K. and Smith, S. (eds) *International Relations Theory Today*. Cambridge: Polity Press, pp. 175–97.

True, J. (1996) 'Feminism'. In Burchill, S. and Linklater, A. *Theories of International Relations*. London: Macmillan, pp. 210–51.

Walker, R.B.J. (1988) *One World, Many Worlds: Struggles for a Just World Peace*. London: Zed Books.

Walt, S. (1991) 'The renaissance of security studies', *International Studies Quarterly*, 35 (2), 211–37.

4

Environmental/Ecological Philosophies and Security

Even before Buzan's landmark contribution (1983) got the security debate going in International Relations (IR) itself, from within the Peace Studies community Johan Galtung, along with others such as Richard Falk and the World Order Models Project, was already arguing that 'the environment is, or should be, a basic aspect of the security debate' and that separating the environment from security was 'the type of segmented thinking that cannot help being harmful to progress in [both] fields' (Galtung, 1982, pp. 99–100). This chapter and the next one move outside IR specific debates and suggest that IR needs to be more open to outside influences in effectively rethinking security. We look at the environment (an increasingly important issue area in broadly defined international studies) and Peace Studies (usually described as a sub-field of IR but a reasonably isolated one). Again, the purpose of these chapters is to suggest new tools for thinking about the third world and the framing of security issues within it. Accordingly, this chapter seeks not an explanation of what environmental security might *mean*, but an *understanding* of how a consideration of the environment can help us *think* more usefully about security, particularly in third world contexts.

A particular reason for including this chapter is that the term 'environmental security' is one which is increasingly used by academics and more so policy-makers, as if it were not only self-evident but also self-evidently good. Particularly at the policy-making level, it is implied that sustainable development/ecological equilibrium (call it what you will) is within our grasp without substantial modification of current forms of human organization. This chapter seeks, primarily, to raise doubts about this certainty and to suggest where the fault lines might be. The argument offered is, basically, that in thinking about different ecological philosophies (or *ecosophies*; see Naess, 1995), we can fundamentally inform our perceptions of what future societies may look like and how security might be attained/guaranteed within them. On the other hand, we may also want to argue that current patterns of human behaviour are the cause of insecurity, as well as holding within them the seeds of further insecurity. A subsidiary argument is that in looking at ecologically motivated resistance we can see strategies for providing security in many community contexts worldwide. This type of argument is more fully developed in Chapter 6 (see also Guha and Martinez-Alier, 1997).

Whilst the end of the Cold War is widely viewed as having 'allowed' environmental issues on to the IR agenda, for many interested in promoting an ecologically secure future this event has less significance than for others (see Buzan, 1995, p. 387); when liberal democracy comprehensively won this 'war', it did so as one system of environmentally destructive industrial society against a rival system of destructive *industrial society* (Bahro, 1994) but a system of destructive industrial society nonetheless (see Dobson, 1995, pp. 29–33). There is a wide range of environmental positions.

In order then to contextualize our consideration of environment and security, this chapter first introduces, briefly and simply, the emergence of a general environmental consciousness in academia and within the population at large, and the reasons for it. As part of this, we also look at the philosophical underpinnings of how human–nature relations have been understood and evolved over time. We do not discuss in detail the differences between environmentalism and ecologism (for an excellent summary, see Dobson, 1995) and the extent to which the former emerged, or (more properly) existed, before the latter. Nor do we detail every signpost on the chronological route.

As alluded to above, an important danger in the security debate is that *security* can become a loose synonym of bad, (Deudney, 1990), and indeed Galtung even mentions sexual frustration in this context (1982, p. 85); accordingly, at this stage we want to demonstrate why and how the environment came to be recognized as an area where some *bad* things were happening (rather than as an infinite supplier of *good* things) as a prelude to a discussion of how thinking about things environmental can help us in thinking about the idea of security.

We then move on to examine the ways in which this environmental consciousness has been incorporated into the various strands of IR, especially in relation to security. That is, we will look not only at how the traditional realist IR community has coped with the increasing international salience of issues that are outside the parameters of its famed elegant simplicity, but also at how other mainstream approaches (liberal and Marxist-derived) have coped with environmental issues. It will subsequently be argued that rather than the environment being something that can be easily tacked on in this manner (though efforts have been made to do so), what may or may not constitute environmental security is something which should be treated as a site of contention and, most fundamentally, as a debate between distinct eco-philosophies. In other words, whilst arguments over what environmental security might be in fact *span* the inter-paradigm debate (see the Introduction) and beyond, for our purposes here it offers another range of theoretical tools with which we may wish to pick at security. The linkages between Northern over-consumption, Southern poverty and global economic structures provide the particular salience for the third world.

The final section of this chapter looks in a little more detail at these theoretical tools and their implications. Whilst various strands of environmental, ecological or green political thought can be described as lying on a *continuum* between what might be characterized as 'adaptive' or 'reformist' and 'restructuring' or 'radical' end-points, these are, more normally, *divided* between two broad types of thinking known as shallow environmental (adaptive/reformist) and deep ecological (restructuring/radical) modes of thought. The extent to which we can put environmentalism and ecologism on the same continuum, rather than dividing them into two entirely separate camps, is considered by Andrew Dobson (1995). His case is that 'environmentalism' is a suffix which can be added to a whole range of ideologies; that is, it is a cross-cutting ideology (hence eco-socialism for instance). However, it is convincingly argued that 'ecologism' represents an ideology in itself; nonetheless, Dobson himself uses a 'minimalist'/'maximalist' distinction within green thought which seems to imply a continuum of sorts and that the image of continuum can operate as a useful heuristic device.[1]

Perceptions of the Environment

Premodern to Modern

Since the 1960s there has apparently been the beginnings of a shift in (Western/academic) perceptions regarding 'the environment' and the 'human–nature' relationship. These have, to some extent, replaced the previous hostile image in which it was the duty of *man* to conquer *his* [*sic*] surroundings and which is reflected, for instance, in the work of Marx (1961). This previous image has its roots in the Enlightenment period and particularly in the work of Francis Bacon and René Descartes; the shift in perceptions of the human–nature relationship from medieval (reverential) to modern conceptualizations (instrumental) saw a huge expansion of human activity at the expense of the non-human realm (see Hovden, 1998). In other words, the scientific revolution was absolutely crucial in instigating a dramatic shift in perceptions.[2]

Prior to this modern period, ideas about improving the human condition (utopian ideas) were connected with conceptions of superior forms of social organization and hence spiritual advancement; with the scientific revolution, however, utopianism became associated with conquest of, and dominion over, the natural world, with the potential of associated positive social implications becoming a major justification of science itself. The fact that 'the spread of what was called "enlightenment" has been the spread of darkness, of the extinction of life and life-enhancing processes' forms the basis of contemporary rethinking of, and concern about, the way humans interact with nature (Shiva, 1988, p. xiv).

Without ever being a brilliant scientist or profound philosopher, Francis Bacon's role in shifting images from the premodern to modern is, nonetheless, highly significant. For instance, he suggested various justifications of science to fit the religious orthodoxy of the time, claiming, for example, that it would be an injury unto the majesty of God only to contemplate the superficial splendour of God's creatures and not to take a closer look (Farrington, 1951; Bacon, 1994). In other words, Bacon found important religious loopholes through which science could pop, and then prosper accordingly. Bacon's commitment to science was highly significant and indeed he died as the result of performing experiments to test hypotheses regarding putrefaction.

However, *intellectually*, far greater credit in this process is due to René Descartes, who established two metaphysical premises of profound influence in Western philosophy. The first was that there was a clear distinction between mind and body and the second, crucial in this context, that the natural world is a machine. In effect, he argued that the understanding of natural processes can be achieved by reducing them to mechanical laws. To Descartes, and those subsequently influenced by him, nature is merely matter in motion; in this way it is thus removed from its mystical medieval status. Nature is no longer alive but dead, it has not intrinsic value but only instrumental use value (Merchant, 1992). This anthropocentrism (human-centredness) asserts that 'there is a clear and morally relevant dividing line between humankind and the rest of nature, that humankind is the only or principal source of value and meaning in the world, and that nonhuman nature is there for no other purpose but to serve mankind' (Eckersley, 1992, p. 51).[3]

We should not overestimate the extent to which this Cartesian view of the human–nature relationship either has been replaced or was able to replace totally what went before. Premodern conceptions of the human–nature relationship do still exist among small, but significant groups of human beings, mainly those whose ancestors were not tracked down by modern science and European 'civilization'. Furthermore, though the effects of industrial society *have* tended towards a process of reverse transformation, it is nonetheless the case that anthropocentrism is still very much the generally predominant mindset amongst Western(ized) populations.[4] However, anthropocentrism *is* now subject to conscious reflection and the physical effects of humans denying and losing sight of how humanity is a part of, and constituted by, nature are becoming increasingly apparent. The debate over whether to resolve a perceived environmental crisis by utilizing a thoroughly renegotiated anthropocentrism (environmentalism), or by replacing it with an ecocentrism (at the heart of ecologism), are at the base of the shallow versus deep ecology arguments.

Post-industrial

In the context of the previous chapter, it is worth noting at this point that 'the ecological challenge, precisely to the extent that it is a critical challenge, can be seen as a renewal of the enlightenment project itself' (Hayward, 1994, p. 39). In other words, just as with Bacon, we are dealing with an appeal to human *reason*; an emancipatory politics that seeks the maximization of the autonomy of human and non-human beings. Thus Enlightenment rationality is not rejected simply on the grounds of its rationality but because it is not enlightened in an environmental context. On the other hand, the technical optimism of environmentalism is much more of a problem-solving than a critical exercise; however, both represent a questioning of the human–nature relationship to some extent.[5]

What is certain is that environmental awareness and conciousness have been fundamentally changing and that the core of much recent green political theory/philosophy has been a problematization of the human/non-human relationship as one in which 'intrinsic value resides exclusively, or at least predominantly, in humans' (Hayward, 1994, p. 2). In the context of the developed world this has been termed a move to post-industrial consciousness. However, the radicalism of Northern environmentalism has frequently been co-opted or has dissipated as the post-industrial movement has grown. Environmental concern has signified little more than nimbyism[6] and problem-solving[7] and, where it has addressed wider issues, has become broadly supportive of the status quo. Hence it has looked for modification of lifestyles in the North whilst urging the South to preserve the environment, even though Northern countries destroyed theirs by development.

In terms of the third world and security, ecocentrism (ecologism) is, for us, more significant since it places the burden of action not entirely with the poorer countries. Shallow approaches have tended to urge the 'third world' to do as we say and not as we did or even are doing. That is, in encouraging a different (or sustainable) development, shallow approaches tend to suggest the preservation of the vast resources of the South for Northern use, whereas deep greens more readily acknowledge the role of the North and its high consumption practices as *the* primary cause of environmental degradation. As Leslie Sklair notes (and we return to such matters in Chapter 7), the 'campaign for "sustainable development" can be interpreted...as an attempt to shore up some idea of "development" against [a] critical tide of cultural survivalism, eco-feminism and ecophilosophy' (1991, p. 220). On the other hand, US deep greens in particular have been accused of eco-imperialism for their obsession with wilderness and inability to recognize that many anthropocentric problems should take precedence over blind eco-centrism. However, in questioning industrial society deep green approaches do offer hope for an alternative to modernization, globalization and destruction of cultures and communities (Guha and Martinez-Alier, 1997). This developing debate and its implications for security are returned to later.

Reasons for This Developing Consciousness and Debate

Environmental concerns themselves are not especially new and examples may be found from history of environmental disasters and environmental laws. Plato complained of soil exhaustion because of agricultural practices (McCormick, 1989), the people of Easter Island turned their well-resourced island paradise into a cultish, cannibalistic nightmare (refuting the myth that our ancestors possessed some innate ability to manage resources which we have lost with modernity) (Bahro, 1994, p. 24), and both British and US history are full of examples of anti-pollution concerns and laws (Neuzil and Kovarik, 1996, pp. 173–6).

However, with the industrial revolution, and the increasing concentration of people in cities, we can see the beginnings of a popular consciousness regarding the issue which has burgeoned, along with the exponential reach of technology, in the latter part of the twentieth century. It is only latterly that the 'wisdom' of human progress has been questioned to any great extent. In a sense arbitrarily, the beginnings (and we are still really at the beginning) of the fundamental shift in consciousness away from a blinkered Cartesian view of the human–nature relationship is associated with Rachel Carson's seminal work *Silent Spring*, a 'pesticide danger' novel first published in 1962 (Carson, 1965). We suggest this to be an arbitrary date since it post-dates a lot of environmentalism's concerns dating from the industrial revolution (Neuzil and Kovarik, 1996), but pre-dates a fully developed ecologism.[8] Since that time, and contrary to perceptions held in the industrial age (if we assume we are now in some kind of post-industrial era), the environment has become perceived as being vital to the existence of humanity rather than a limitless, often hostile and external, resource to be exploited for the production of human wealth.

Various factors have contributed to growing public awareness of the issues at stake; regrettably, though inevitably, these factors include highly publicized environmental disasters such as those at the nuclear reactors of Three Mile Island in the United States in 1979 and Chernobyl, Ukraine, in 1986, as well as the human tragedy caused by gas leaks at the Union Carbide factory at Bhopal, India, in 1984 (Thomas, 1992). Through these and other less publicized 'accidents', it is becoming increasingly apparent that life is characterized by risk and that environmental risks are particularly associated with the current organization of the global economy and societies.

Interest really began to pick up in the early 1970s; it is at this time that there took place in Stockholm in 1972 the United Nations Conference on the Human Environment (UNCHE), explicitly linking environment and development themes for the first time. The same year saw the publication of various doom-laden predictions about the future, most notably the Club of Rome's *Limits to Growth* report (Meadows et al., 1972). This report was significant in that the researchers used computer-modelling techniques to 'prove' their findings; to the extent that they have not been proven,[9] this represents another failure of the so-called behavioural revolution in the social sciences. However, the report had, and continues to have, a significant influence in stimulating discussion, debate and research.

Despite the influence that various events, reports and books were having amongst the population at large, in the very tense times of the Cold War, we should remind ourselves at this point that all this had little effect in strategic (security) studies in IR. Rather as it is difficult to remember what the cold of winter is *really* like from the sunshine of a hot summer's day, it is correspondingly easy to underestimate, from the perspective of today, the extent to which considerations of the Cold War dominated academic debate within IR and, theoretically, what a liberated time the 1990s have actually been, despite the (concealed) intellectual baggage which people still carry.[10] Thus, although a public environmental consciousness built up during the 1970s and 1980s,[11] it is not really until the end of the Cold War that IR began to think about environmental issues, and latterly environmental philosophies, in a much more serious way (see, for instance, Hovden, 1998).

The overarching nature of environmental concern is such that those interested in security or IR and the environment do not form a separate block. Frequently, they would fall into the categories realist, neorealist, critical security theorist and so on. Without wishing to rehash either the statistics surrounding environmental degradation and its transboundary effects or the often pious injunctions to action made by politicians and academics alike,[12] it is nonetheless the case that the environment has become a very important part of the international relations agenda in recent years and that within International Relations (the discipline) it has become an important area of study. The particular way that sustainable development fits into this picture, from its original formulation by the International Union for the Conservation of Nature (IUCN) in 1980, through its appropriation by the Brundtland Commission (1987) and then the Rio Conference of 1992 and Rio +5 in 1997, is dealt with more fully in Chapter 7.

With the increasing importance of this issue area, the various theoretical schools have sought to demonstrate how they incorporate the environment into their analysis of IR and security. Accordingly, this chapter now seeks to outline the various approaches that have been, and can be, taken to environmental security. In effect, the environment as a security issue has come to mean how do we deal with this vital component of our existence, a remarkably contentious point as it turns out and one which has turned environmental diplomacy into political manoeuvring more than serious environmental protection (Susskind, 1994). As will be seen, different environmental philosophies provide us with different ways in which we might then view security from an environmental standpoint.

Mainstream International Relations and the Environment

Realists, such as Morgenthau, or neorealists, such as Waltz, who liken the separation of the international political realm from other realms as necessary for greater understanding to the way that economics was previously separated from other realms, would argue that there is no special need to consider the environment in IR. They would argue that their realism and neorealism respectively capture the essence of international politics, that any definition they offer of security, whilst not dealing with environmental problems, is the proper subject matter of IR, and that except as it impinges in certain ways on IR, the study of the environment can safely be left to biologists and ecologists.

Thus realists have preoccupied themselves with national access to strategically important raw materials (for example, oil) or renewable resources (particularly water) but not specifically with issues such as conservation of particular species or geological features or the effects of poverty on the environment. As the cumulative effects of environmental problems have become apparent, some realists have been reluctant to admit that this has any implications for their simplified essence of world politics despite convincing work done to demonstrate the contrary (see for example, Westing, 1988). In a sense then, realists argue that realism has always dealt with the environment. Realists have considered aspects such as geography and natural resources in their definitions of power (Morgenthau, 1978), and the possibility of conflict being caused by disagreements over the environment is easily incorporated into analysis (Homer-Dixon, 1991, 1994). Spykman's *America's Strategy in World*

Politics: The United States and the Balance of Power (1942) is one of the earliest realist accounts and reflects the awareness of the importance of access to raw materials in international relations.

A realist rejection of re-defining security is not, however, simply based on the perception that realism has effectively dealt with such issues alone but that new approaches are actually dangerous in many ways; realism's parsimonious concentration on essence (regarded as elegantly simplistic) is necessary in order to focus the mind, lest it lose itself in the complexity of all things social and the full richness of human existence. It has been argued that 'if we continue to broaden our definition, then security/insecurity will remain what international relations is all about, but this will offer no coherent focus' (Morgan, 1992, p. 465). Morgan goes on to argue that we should avoid this; if we fail to focus on what security is, at base, all about, the inherent dangers will be enormous. Put simply, a realist might suggest that we can only worry about global warming if we are sure that nuclear winter is not just around the corner.

Realists then are either happy that their definition of security has ample scope for incorporating the environment or sceptical, even worried, about the idea of extending the concept. The latter group have allies in various environmentally concerned authors who argue that trying to absorb the idea of environment, defined more fundamentally than raw materials, into a firmly established concept such as national security will hinder efforts to provide any level of environmental security, meaning stability, certainty or liveability for human beings. (Deudney, 1990, 1991). In doing so, the importance of environmental problems is not denied; it is simply argued that because of the different sorts of threats presented by environmental issues (unintentionally caused, long time-frame and requiring concerted international efforts to resolve them) relative to military threats, it is best not to try and squeeze the environment into existing notions of security. However, as David Campbell has noted, this is exactly what has happened; 'the effort to address environmental issues within the parameters of international relations and national security often involves simply extending the old register of security to cover this new domain' (1992, p. 257),[13] although it might be argued that early efforts to raise the profile of environmental problems have done this intentionally in an effort to get them more seriously addressed (for example, Mathews, 1989).

As the previous chapter has shown, for some theorists of IR, theories can be divided into two sorts which we might want to call problem-solving and critical theories. For the latter, what unites mainstream IR theories is much more important than what divides them, notwithstanding the contribution of Marxism to certain critical theories. To such a view the fierce debate between neorealism and neoliberal institutionalism is virtually irrelevant;[14] however, for those involved in the debate (which has seen idealism re-enter IR), it is of the utmost significance. For those who see world politics in more pluralistic terms, environmental issues form part of an increasingly complex agenda in which not only states but also scientific epistemic communities (see Haas, 1990), international governmental organizations (IGOs) and non-governmental organizations (NGOs) play an important role in shaping policy and, where necessary, arranging international treaties through environmental diplomacy (Susskind, 1994).

In effect, such work as this rekindles the idea of providing (environmental) security through international co-operation based on common interest, and implies acceptance of the existing arrangements of states in a global political economy and the possibility of reform to ameliorate the most deleterious environmental effects that it provokes. It would be argued, by advocates of a pluralist institutionalist path to environmental security, that the (only) other choice – unrestrained selfish behaviour on the part of states – can ultimately lead only to ecological disaster and possibly our extinction as a species.[15]

For Marx the environment did not really enter into his analysis – certainly not the idea of environmental problems as an ultimately limiting factor for production. This has provided the basis for some of the tensions between radical green and radical left analyses; in the early days of environmental concern, many on the left saw environmental concern as an upper-class fad or another establishment trick which would freeze local and global inequalities.

However, both with time and with attention paid to some common roots in certain forms of (utopian and anarchist) socialism, some similarities between red and green have emerged, giving rise to 'traffic light coalitions'.[16] Hence, for Marxist-influenced or derived theories within IR today, the environment (and eco-centric challenges) certainly presents greater 'problems' than it did for Marx. As noted, perhaps the biggest of these problems is that in accepting the existence of environmental limits there is always the danger of freezing existing patterns of wealth distribution; the similarities of the words 'conservation' and 'conservative' are thus worrying for many left-leaning thinkers. However, in striving to close such gaps by increased production there is the risk that ultimately an even worse situation will be provoked. These problems feed into the whole North–South issue and a range of ethical questions of responsibility both for current environmental problems and their resolution and for equity now and in the future. Ultimately, the debate boils down to a series of questions concerning the extent to which human emancipation is a pre-condition for the emancipation of nature and whether exploitation of the planet inevitably involves exploitation of people (see Pepper, 1996).

Thus the environment feeds into various mainstream accounts of IR in different ways. Explicitly or implicitly, it also informs, or merits consideration by, various critical and postmodern contributions to the social sciences and IR's security debate (see Jagtenberg and McKie, 1997). For instance, David Campbell argues that 'as a danger which can be articulated in terms of security strategies that are deterritorialised, involve communal co-operation and refigure economic relationships, the environment can serve to enframe a different reading of the political' (1992, p. 257).

On the basis of the foregoing, we might want to accept that it is not a terribly useful exercise to try and squeeze the environment into a single conception of environmental security nor, following Deudney (1991), to squeeze environmental issues into already existing concepts such as national security. We would further want to stress here that there are clearly serious environmental problems in international relations that need resolution and that we might be better to regard environmental security as an area of debate apart from national or traditional security concerns.

Eco-philosophy and the Third World: The Significance of Deep and Shallow Approaches

In looking then at security and the third world, we argue here for the need to look at the philosophical underpinnings of proposed methods for resolving environmental problems. Here we encounter huge differences of opinion regarding the best way to solve environmental problems or to stave off ecological tragedy, some of which have been alluded to above. Environmental security, in our view, rests not with how it is adopted by IR theorists, but which eco-philosophy ultimately underlies attitudes within communities and societies. In thinking about the relationship between human beings and nature, we can begin to envisage more and less secure futures based on how this relationship is perceived and how it develops.[17] We move on now to consider ecological philosophy in a little more detail.[18]

Our overview up to this point now brings us to some fundamental points. What we want to argue for is the notion that rather than incorporate various environmental *issues* into IR and security in various ways, if we are talking about the third world we need to think about how various eco-philosophies inform various positions and how this can help us to *rethink* security. If, as we have argued in Chapter 1, we understand the third world as those marginalized in some sense we can see intimate links between these people, communities and states and with environmental degradation. It is often stated, but true, that the poor frequently 'cause' environmental degradation because of the survival-first strictures in which they are forced to exist. What we are suggesting here, therefore, is that debates over eco-philosophy can significantly inform the security debate.

Western Enlightenment reason was able to overturn environmental management practices, utilized by indigenous peoples throughout the world, which had evolved over time and (usually) passed the test of usefulness; the environmental, and associated human, tragedies of peanut production in Africa or banana production in Central America, for instance, are the results of reason and its application in the guise of development destroying traditional knowledge and strategies to provide security in the process (see Chapter 6). Such activities, controlled by Western corporations, investments and interests provide insecure jobs with associated health risks, throw peasants from the land and force them to over-exploit what is left; such activities poison the land with pesticides or exhaust it but are essential to the primary product economies of poorer countries.

Now that flaws have been spotted in the above – and now that it has been suggested that it is unsustainable – which eco-philosophy will inform the response? Up to the present the answer is that the same faith in a particular development philosophy that created the problem is also suggested as the solution. Anthropocentric environmentalism suggests that we can tinker with the current system providing sustainable development. Even its advocates suggest that this will *not* provide security for everyone but prosperity for the majority. Sustainable development is thus embraced but what progress is made? More resources continue to be used though more efficiently. Conservation is also embraced. As well as depriving many of their traditional lifestyles, what does this do? Where tropical forest products are not imported on environmental grounds, ancient forests can also make way for soya – highly demanding on soil and not subject to such import restrictions. The refusal to face up to basic issues of human organization and lifestyles can lead to all sorts of anomalies such as this and there are no signs that environmental indicators are improving or that human misery is decreasing.

It is no longer acceptable to dismiss radical environmentalism (ecologism) as eco-fascist, conservative or just plain hippy. The practical problems are difficult to resolve, but in considering the problems of security and the third world, thinking about eco-philosophy and how it informs global political economy and ecology can tell us much about the reasons for insecurity.

Dobson (1995) provides an excellent introduction to many different sorts of ecological thought and the differences between environmentalism and ecologism, but perhaps the simplest categorization is to divide them between 'shallow' and 'deep' ecological approaches. As we have seen, these terms are sometimes known, respectively, as reformism and radicalism. Shallow ecology, as its name suggests, does not imply profound changes in the forms of human social organization. Shallow ecology is about managing the effects of industrialization and allowing human society to 'progress' in much the same way that it has been doing; 'environmentalism argues for a managerial approach to environmental problems, secure in the belief that they can be solved without fundamental changes in present values or patterns of production and consumption' (Dobson, 1995, p. 1). On the other hand, deep ecology, or eco-centrism (O'Riordan, 1976; Eckersley, 1992), rejects the anthropocentrism currently practised and demands radical changes in forms of socio-political organization, including respect for non-human species. It argues that the relationship between humans and nature, as mediated by modern science, largely explains the current environmental crisis and that various facets of this relationship need to be fundamentally restructured – that is if the planet and all its inhabitants are to enjoy a secure future.

In effect, within a shallow approach there *is* room for an argument over global inequality and the role of international, especially North–South, relations. Some shallow approaches will want to point to the ways in which this relationship, with its extremes of poverty and wealth, is contributing to ecological breakdown, though there will be differences of interpretation regarding how to deal with this. On the other hand, for deep ecologists, to concentrate on one aspect of oppression (whether it is North–South based, gender based and so on) is to miss the fundamental points of the impossibility of growth in a finite system and the lack of respect offered the non-human world by the human; 'ecologism makes the earth as physical object the very foundation stone of its intellectual edifice, arguing that its finitude is the basic reason why infinite population and economic growth are impossible and why, consequently, profound changes in our social and political behaviour need to take place' (Dobson, 1995, p. 16). The inherent optimism in shallow approaches regarding the possibility of using reform to solve environmental problems and end human misery is rejected.

There is much misunderstanding surrounding deep ecology. This is not least because its privileging of the oppression of nature over other oppressions combined with a recognition that the environment could be protected *without* genuine participatory democracy has led to accusations of eco-fascism. However, these accusations are refuted by ecologism, not only because it claims to be an ideology which cannot be tacked on to others in this manner but also because 'the very *idea* of dominating nature stems from the domination of human by human' so that the latter must be effectively challenged as part of a radical ecological project (Bookchin, 1991, p. 131). As its proponents have pointed out, deep ecology need not be a fixed position but generally involves a belief in the intrinsic value of non-human life, a distinction between vital and non-vital needs and the conclusion that human interference in the natural world is currently infringing the vital needs of many other species. It suggests the need for fundamental changes in society's economic, technological and ideological structures, a belief in the difference between improving quality of life and constantly improving living standards, and an active commitment towards implementing the changes necessary to a deep green future.

In the context of ecological critiques it is perhaps ironic that Linklater (1990) criticizes realism in IR for working within limits rather than pushing them in order to secure change. To the extent that radical green perspectives form a part of the critical security agenda of IR, it is precisely to argue against the constant pushing of limits which has accompanied human existence at least since the Enlightenment. However, this is no more than semantics since the limits to which Linklater refers are those of human perception of what is possible and what disempowers us; ecological perspectives, in making us aware of physical limits, are also urging us to think beyond mental barriers and our addiction to the 'mega-machine' of industrial society in order to create a radical green society (Bahro, 1994).

Conclusions

Thus, in terms of the third world, shallow (reformist) environmentalism *might* encourage debate about the role of poorer countries and acknowledges poverty as an important cause of environmental degradation; it *can* stress the crucial responsibility of Northern countries in helping Southern countries to develop richer, more equitable societies whilst at the same time providing respect for the global environment. This debate opens up fundamental questions about the structuring of the global economy. However, shallow environmentalism is more frequently used to justify existing relationships, even if couched in different rhetoric. It insists that the current system more or less works and can be successfully reformed and that within this reform there is still a (single) developmental truth which third world countries can follow in order to catch up. In terms of their security, especially if we accept a broadened agenda, this means demanding of third world countries that they seek to imitate first world success without doing the same things and in a world where the space to cast an ecological shadow no longer exists as it did for the developed world.[19] However, attempting to develop in the same way will undoubtedly place further pressure on global ecological systems. Consequently, shallow environmentalism can best be seen as a way of protecting Northern lifestyles and enshrining, in perpetuity, insecurity in the third world.

On the other hand, deep ecology envisages a radically different world which would create bio-communities. A deep ecological future would require a fundamental transformation of our spirituality regarding the planet (see Dobson, 1995; Bahro, 1994; Porritt, 1984). This would lead to a de-emphasis on material things and liberal individualism and a (re)emphasis on living within limits. Over time populations would have to drop,[20] and peoples would live in sustainable communities, similar in some respects but culturally diverse. The linkages to certain forms of anarchism and utopian socialism are evident and so is the conclusion that any geographical or other notion of the third world would become obsolete. However, despite the ultimate 'secure' destination, the utopian romanticism of deep ecological perspectives seems to translate into a call for a 'happy ever after' scenario without an appropriate plan of action to bring this about. Vogler is right to say that how to achieve such deep green futures is problematical; 'although there is much force in the radical [ecological] critique, it is one thing to argue that the scale of global change requires a complete reversal of the economic growth trajectory allied to a total overhaul of the international system, and quite another to contemplate it as practical politics' (1996, pp. 217–18). In other words, deep ecological prescriptions frequently tend towards the unrealistic, and even uncaring in the sense that very real human problems are subsumed in the call for biocentrism. The idea that rather than an eco-paradise we might adapt nature whilst maintaining its balance seems frequently lost.

Returning in a sense to the idea of environmental thought as a continuum, Tim Hayward tries to inject a certain optimism that shallow and deep ecology need not be envisaged as simply a stark contrast between rich world tinkering and rich world dreaming respectively. He argues that the 'shallow' lifestyle changes made by many ordinary people (recycling, car-sharing and so on) 'can be seen as part of a broader strategy to transform and enrich the very concept of the political, and thereby to increase the sense, and reality, of empowerment of those hitherto excluded from politics in its mainstream definition' (Hayward, 1994, p. 196). In doing so, Hayward is able to avoid the status quo labelling of shallow approaches and the objections to a more radical philosophy that it is impossible and, perhaps, dangerous dreaming.[21] Writing from an environmental/ecological perspective, he thus draws up alongside critical security theorist Campbell (1992) in seeing the linkages between the environment as an issue area and the environment as new framings of the political that do not suffer from the marginalization which we have used here to define the third world.

Notes

1. In the next chapter see, for example, David Dunn's (1978) maximalist/minimalist continuum used to describe the postitive/negative peace relationship within Peace Studies.
2. In terms of arguments regarding the anthropocentrism of modern societies, it should also be noted here that 'the ascendency of enlightenment rationality was in large measure due to purging anthropocentric assumptions and methods from science' (Hayward, 1994, p. 6).
3. In the context of this section in particular, my personal thanks are due to Eivind Hovden.
4. Some would argue that androcentrism would be more appropriate in this case.
5. As Hayward puts it, 'green political theory involves the pursuit not of absolute novelty in conceptualising society and politics but a thoroughgoing critique of dominant conceptions of the political in the light of ecological considerations' (1994, p. 196).
6. 'Nimby' is an acronym signifying Not In My Back Yard.
7. Characterized by recycling, more efficient cars and so on.

8. Dobson (1995), for instance, suggests that *Silent Spring* is part of the pre-conditions for a fully eco-centric position which can be more properly dated from Meadows *et al.* (1972). In other words, environmentalism and its myths persisted until it was 'proved' that the system needed overhauling rather than tinkering with.
9. Various scenarios, some more optimistic than others, have all predicted exhaustion of key resources and imminent collapse of the growth model.
10. Postmodernists would no doubt contest this idea of 'theoretical liberation', arguing that most scholars are still positivistically imprisoned, but the fact that postmodernism has seriously engaged with IR, and vice versa, supports the contention.
11. The role of various United Nations commissions, the United Nations Environment Programme (UNEP), demands for a new international economic order (NIEO) at the United Nations General Assembly and so on are significant but are not explored here.
12. For example, British Prime Minister Tony Blair's speech at the Rio +5 meeting of the United Nations General Assembly, 16 to 27 June 1997. See newspapers of the time, including the *Guardian*, for comment.
13. Campbell does not use the convention of this book of referring to International Relations the discipline with upper-case initial letters; this occasionally leads to ambiguity.
14. This debate has achieved particular prominence in the US academic community and is basically one over the extent to which states are able to co-operate to achieve their aims in the context of an anarchic state system.
15. Those within the neorealist/neoliberal squabble seem not to recognize multiple theories and even paradigms in IR but rather the paramountcy of their argument of emphasis over the possibility and desirability of co-operation in international relations (see Smith, 1995).
16. For example, in Germany at local (Berlin) and national levels but also localized alliances in many parts of the world.
17. On the need for fundamental shifts away from reliance on the mega-machine of industrial capitalism, see Bahro (1994).
18. The whole environment and security debate is much more complex than can be incorporated in a chapter of this length. For further reading, see, for instance, Tennberg (1995), Stern (1995), Vogler (1993), Mathews (1989), Imber (1991) and Holst (1989) amongst many others.
19. This basically refers to the fact that the developed world became so and is so because of its exploitation of other areas of the planet. For a discussion of the notion of ecological shadow, see Conca, Alberty and Dabelko (1995).
20. This does not represent an invitation to genocide as is suggested by Mike Simons in talking about the prescriptions of Paul Ehrlich in *Green Line*, No. 64, July/August 1988, quoted in Dobson (1995, p. 19).
21. Dangerous in the sense that attempts to institute such a society would likely be fraught with all sorts of dangers of social chaos.

References

Bacon, F. (1994) *Novum Organum*. Translated and edited by P.Urbach and J. Gibson. Chicago: Open Court.

Environmental/Ecological Philosophies 91

Bahro, R. (1994) *Avoiding Social and Ecological Disaster: The Politics of World Transformation*. London: Gateway Books.

Bookchin M. (1991) 'Where I stand now'. In Bookchin, M. and Foreman, D. *Defending the Earth*. Montreal: Black Rose Books.

Brundtland, G. (1987) *Our Common Future*. Oxford: Oxford University Press. World Commission on Environment and Development, The Brundtland Report.

Buzan, B. (1983) *People, States and Fear: The National Security Problem in International Relations*, 1st edition. Brighton: Wheatsheaf.

Buzan, B. (1995) 'The present as a historic turning point', *Journal of Peace Research*, 30 (4), 385–98.

Campbell, D. (1992) *Writing Security*. Manchester: Manchester University Press.

Carson, R. (1965) *Silent Spring*. Harmondsworth: Penguin.

Conca, K., Alberty, M. and Dabelko, G. (1995) *Green Planet Blues*. Boulder, CO: Westview Press.

Deudney, D. (1990) 'The case against linking environmental degradation and national security', *Millennium: Journal of International Studies*, 19 (3), 461–76.

Deudney, D. (1991) 'Environment and security: muddled thinking', *Bulletin of Atomic Scientists*, 47 (3), 22–8.

Dobson, A. (1995) *Green Political Thought*, 2nd edition. London: Routledge.

Dunn, D. (1978) 'Peace research'. In Taylor, T. (ed.) *Theories of International Relations*. London: Longmans, pp. 257–79.

Eckersley, R. (1992) *Environmentalism and Political Theory: Towards an Ecocentric Approach*. London: UCL Press.

Farrington, B. (1951) *Francis Bacon: Philosopher of Industrial Science*. London: Lawrence and Wishart.

Galtung, J. (1975–80) *Essays in Peace Research (Volumes One to Five)*. Copenhagen: Christian Ejlers.

Galtung, J. (1982) *Environment, Development and Military Activity: Towards Alternative Security Doctrines*. Oslo: Universitetsforlaget.

Gleick, P. (1991) 'Environment and security: the clear connections', *Bulletin of Atomic Scientists*, 47 (3), 16–21.

Guha, R. and Martinez-Alier, J. (1997) *Environmentalism: North and South*. London: Routledge.

Haas, P. (1990) *Saving the Mediterranean: The Politics of International Environmental Cooperation*. New York: Columbia University Press.

Hayward, T. (1994) *Ecological Thought: An Introduction*. Oxford: Polity Press.

Holst, J. (1989) 'Security and the environment: a preliminary exploration', *Bulletin of Peace Proposals*, 20 (2), 123–8.

Homer-Dixon, T. (1991) 'Environmental change and acute conflict', *International Security*, 16 (2), 76–116.

Homer-Dixon, T. (1994) 'Environmental scarcities and violent conflict: evidence from cases', *International Security*, 19 (1), 5–40.

Hovden, E. (1998) *The Problem of Anthropocentrism: A Critique of Institutionalist, Marxist and Reflective International Relations Theoretical Approaches to Environment and Development*. PhD thesis, University of London.

Imber, M. (1991) 'Environmental security: a task for the UN system', *Review of International Studies*, 17 (2), 201–12.

Jagtenberg, T. and McKie, D. (1997) *Eco-impacts and the Greening of Postmodernity: New Maps for Communication Studies, Cultural Studies, and Sociology*. London: Sage.

Krause, K. and Williams, M. (eds) (1997) *Critical Security Studies: Concepts and Cases*. London: UCL Press.

Linklater, A. (1990) *Beyond Realism and Marxism: Critical Theory and International Relations*. London: Macmillan.

Marx, K. (1961) *Capital*. London: Lawrence and Wishart.

Mathews, J. (1989) 'Redefining security', *Foreign Affairs*, 68 (2), 162–77.

McCormick, J. (1989) *Reclaiming Paradise: The Global Environmental Movement*. Bloomington: Indiana University Press.

Meadows, D. *et al.* (1972) *The Limits to Growth*. Washington, DC: Potomac Associates.

Merchant, R. (1992) *Radical Ecology*. London: Routledge.

Morgan, P. (1992) 'Safeguarding security studies', *Arms Control*, 13 (2), 464–79.

Morgenthau, H. (1978) *Politics among Nations: The Struggle for Power and Peace*, 5th edition. New York: Alfred Knopf.

Naess, A. 'The deep ecological movement: some philosophical aspects'. In Sessions, G. (ed.) (1995) *Deep Ecology for the 21st Century*. London: Shambhala, pp. 64–84.

Neuzil, M. and Kovarik, W. (1976) *Mass Media and Environmental Conflict: America's Green Crusades*. London: Sage.

O'Riordan, T. (1976) *Environmentalism*. London: Pion.

Porritt, J. (1984) *Seeing Green*. Oxford: Blackwell.

Pepper, D. (1996) *Modern Environmentalism: An Introduction*. London: Routledge.

Shiva, V. (1988) *Staying Alive: Women, Ecology and Development*. London: Zed Books.

Sklair, L. (1991) *Sociology of the Global System*. London: Harvester Wheatsheaf.

Smith, S. (1995) 'The self-images of a discipline: a geography of international relations theory'. In Booth, K. and Smith, S. (eds) *International Relations Theory Today*. Oxford: Polity Press, pp. 1–37.

Spykman, N. (1942) *America's Strategy in World Politics: The United States and the Balance of Power*. New York: Harcourt, Brace.

Stern, E. (1995) 'Bringing the environment in: the case for comprehensive security', *Cooperation and Conflict*, 30 (3), 211–37.

Susskind, L. (1994) *Environmental Diplomacy: Negotiating More Effective Global Agreements*. Oxford: Oxford University Press.

Tennberg, M. (1995) 'Risky business: defining the concept of environmental security', *Cooperation and Conflict*, 30 (3), 239–58.

Thomas, C. (1992) *The Environment in International Relations*. London: Royal Institute of International Affairs.

Vogler, J. (1993) 'Security and global environmental change', *Conflict Processes*, 1 (2), 15–23.

Vogler, J. (1996) 'The politics of the global environment'. In Bretherton, C. and Ponton, G. *Global Politics: An Introduction*. Oxford: Blackwell, pp. 194–220.

Waltz, K. (1959) *Man, the State and War: A Theoretical Analysis*. London: Columbia University Press.

Westing, A. (1988) 'The military sector vis-à-vis the environment', *Journal of Peace Research*, 25 (3), 257–64.

5

Engaging with Other Fields and Disciplines

Other than introducing the idea of rethinking both security and the third world, this book has so far outlined how security evolved *within* the orthodoxy of IR (Chapter 2), how it is breaking free of that orthodoxy (Chapter 3) and how the widened agenda of IR in the post-Cold War has seen debate over how at least one 'new' issue, that of the environment. It was argued that this might inform the security debate or at least that the philosophical underpinnings of green political thought might influence our thinking on security (Chapter 4). Before looking at how some of these influences have affected our own work on security and (sustainable) development (Chapters 6 and 7) this chapter suggests that 'security' should never have been so jealously guarded by IR and that the discipline will have to deal much more openly with others in the future. Since IR has increasingly been reacting to other disciplines, and influenced by them, this is a matter of inevitability rather than choice.

The basic argument of this chapter is a simple one; that disciplines related to, and even sub-fields of, IR have much to offer to, and exchange with, IR in the development of a broader, more satisfactory security debate. For this purpose, and noting the contribution of authors such as Shaw (1993) who have argued for a more sociological approach to security studies, we focus in this chapter on the historical development and insights of Peace Studies (PS) to demonstrate the significance of that area's work in terms of changing security agendas and the third world. We also note briefly the increasing influences that ideas of security are having in the work of political geographers, already connected to IR by the broader field of international studies.

Beginning with PS we find ourselves entirely in agreement with Australian peace researcher Peter Lawler (1990, p. 126) when he says that 'in reconstructing and extending the concept of security beyond the confines of strategic studies and military thinking, it can draw upon the fields of world order studies, international relations, politics, sociology, global political economy, historical sociology and cultural studies'. However, we do not seek here to discuss the full range of possible influences upon a new security agenda, having already looked at one (environmental philosophy) not mentioned by Lawler, but to focus particularly on PS as a way of demonstrating how the insularity of Cold War IR prevented engagement with influences with the potential to lead to a much more informed, inclusive and interesting debate. The final section of the chapter mentions quite briefly the kinds of *contribution* of Political Geography to IR (and vice versa) and especially the kinds of potential linkages which might be useful to both disciplines in thinking about and understanding security. This is basically an explicit recognition of immanent trends rather than the invention or uncovering of something new.

Peace Studies

PS has a history nearly as long as IR itself, along with some similar roots in idealist thought (see Smith, 1986). It is regarded as a sub-field of the discipline, though in practice it has often seemed to be a rather fenced-off one. This section will first outline the historical development of PS to show its connection to, and separateness from, IR. This separateness was based above all on the realist definition of security; the realist paradox that if you want peace you should prepare for war has always been somewhat anathema to the normative commitments of peace researchers, if not in the closely related area of conflict research. In the course of outlining the history of PS, it will hopefully be demonstrated that questions concerning the concept of security (that IR developed in the 1980s) had, in fact, been largely taken on board by PS in the 1960s during its own radical reconsideration of its core term or idea, peace. This intends to show that this sub-field was well ahead of the game in the security debate, without being explicit about it, and that perhaps Buzan (1983) was lucky in touching a nerve in IR that Galtung and others had failed to do previously.[1] It might also be reiterated here that Buzan may simply have presented his ideas in a way which was much more palatable to an entrenched conservative orthodoxy.

The second half of the chapter then looks at PS today and at the sorts of directions in which it is going. The contention that the PS 'agenda has acquired the qualities of an intellectual black hole'

(Lawler, 1990, p. 110) will be considered, but we nonetheless think that this should show that the peace agenda sits comfortably with a broadened security agenda and the kind of social theoretical influences to which it has been subject (Shaw, 1993). One might argue that PS itself needs a more focused critical approach, but, in effect, we will be arguing for an expanded peace and security studies which will bring PS in from the margins of IR, where it has so far significantly failed to cross-fertilize with the discipline to any serious extent.[2] This will also argue for giving PS credit for the introduction of sociological and other influences in developing the idea of peace from the 1960s onwards which even now could play an important role in helping to think about security as a concept.

A Brief History of Peace Studies

Despite relatively strong links *to* IR, PS did not develop *from* any particular discipline and has no recognized methodology of its own. Its distinctiveness comes solely from a preoccupation with the idea of peace. With a multi-disciplinary background, PS does have its own recognized and respected journals such as the *Journal of Conflict Resolution* and the *Journal of Peace Research*; and, notably, the latter now has a 'sister' publication called *Security Dialogue* (with the former more theoretically orientated). PS can also be said to have a geographically dispersed group of academics who identify with it, annual conferences, as well as university courses and departments, such as that at Bradford in the United Kingdom. There are also international institutes, such as the Stockholm International Peace Research Institute (SIPRI) in Sweden and the Peace Research Institute Oslo (PRIO) in Norway, which attract considerable outside backing and are well respected for the work they do. Rather like IR itself, PS has become extraordinarily diverse, connected as it is by being 'an intellectual enterprise devoted to the study of peace and bringing about a state of peace in human society' (Dunn, 1978, p. 257) and an initial normative attachment to a number of fundamental understandings. Namely, these are that peace is natural, that war is to be avoided and that pacifism is a virtue. PS has rarely exhibited the same level of rigid orthodoxy as IR, but in the sense of this normative commitment now retains a unity (in diversity) which IR has lost.

As with much else in IR as a whole, PS has its roots in a desire to avoid any repetition of the horrors of the First World War. However, PS developed from the work of its own 'founding fathers' and followed a rather different trajectory to that of mainstream IR. The 'founding fathers' or, more correctly, pioneers of research into peace were Lewis Fry Richardson in the United Kingdom and Quincy Wright in the United States. In the inter-war period, both sought to understand war in an effort to control it. Richardson's work was a detailed study of the dynamics of conflicts and arms races (see Richardson, 1960) and Wright conducted similar research in the United States (see Wright, 1942). Their work was highly influential in terms of the ideas and attitudes it developed in their own students; they planted the seeds of PS and, in a somewhat macabre way, these were fertilized by the Second World War and the advent of the atomic bomb. Indeed, many scientists, motivated by their sense of collective guilt and disturbed by the lack of an ethical basis to modern science, have become linked to PS, even founding their own influential journal, the *Bulletin of Atomic Scientists*. Ironically, this was happening at the same time as IR itself was eschewing ethical foreign policy, becoming dominated by a belief in ostensibly *scientific* unchanging laws which made such policy impossible.

Nevertheless, PS, as a sub-field of IR, was not entirely immune to such a trend. Like IR the purpose of some PS altered subtly from a concern to avoid war to one of preventing it *as much as possible*. By the early 1960s there was a thriving PS community, especially in the United States, but normative commitments seemed gently marginalized, though not excluded. The *Journal of Conflict Resolution* was founded at the University of Michigan in the mid-1950s and PS proved highly attractive for those seeking a way out of the Cold War. Whilst in the United Kingdom this *did* mean links with groups such as the Campaign for Nuclear Disarmament (CND), in the United States, motivated by available funding, PS became very establishment orientated. It studied the Cold War balance and its flashpoints in Berlin, Korea and Hungary, for example, and asked the following basically realist questions. What is deterrence? How does it function? How can disarmament/arms control be achieved?

However, PS 'success' in attracting government research grants and building a recognized core of an international academic community also signalled the start of serious internal criticisms that its links, not only to government but also to business, had seen it become sterile, remote and conservative. In part, as a result of internal debate but also as a result of changes in the real world, PS started to diversify. Whilst IR (and other social sciences) was undergoing its so-called second great debate over methodology (the behavioural revolution), PS was also concerned with questions of purpose and ontological choices: why and what to study. A strong European (particularly Scandinavian) PS emerged to counter a more conservative North American current.

The changes in the 'real world' which most influenced PS were first that the early 1960s were the time of the Soviet leader Khrushchev and his ideas of 'peaceful coexistence' with the West; the nuclear war that many had seen as imminent, if not quite inevitable, had apparently been avoided. When the world came closest to it, during the Cuban Missile Crisis of 1962, the impression may also have been given that any crisis could be resolved without recourse to the use of nuclear weapons. In terms of PS' theoretical development, this was also a time of decolonization in the third world and the popularity of Marxist critiques of the colonial age. This saw more radical notions of peace and PS begin to emerge. In 1964, the *Journal of Peace Research* was set up in Oslo under the editorship of Johan Galtung. Galtung, a sociologist, wanted to see the ideas of peace and violence set in the context of wider socio-economic processes, regarding political violence as a result of deeper social and/or economic problems (see Galtung, 1975–80).

Although it has been suggested that Martin Luther King was the first person to make the distinction between negative and positive peace, Galtung certainly tried to develop this distinction; he regarded positive peace as the integration of human society whereas negative peace was simply the absence of physical violence and war, that is, the traditional concerns of PS. By the late 1960s Galtung had been further influenced by the work of Herman Schmid and other PS radicals in Sweden; Schmid's argument for a shift in focus to suppressed or exploited groups led Galtung to modify his view of positive peace to mean the attainment of social justice and, it has been argued, some PS started to look like an 'open-ended critique of all forms of domination' (see Lawler, 1990, p. 121).

By this stage PS was effectively operating along two broad tracks. For some scholars such as Karl Deutsch the importance of social justice was not denied; however, it was asked, with disarmingly simple logic, how could those killed in a nuclear war enjoy social justice (see Deutsch, 1978). It was, in other words, a question of priorities and the elimination of war as an instrument of statecraft would have to precede peace defined positively. Of course this argument can be, and has been, turned on its head by the suggestion that it is social injustice which is most likely to lead to conflict of a physically violent nature, with all its implications. Conflicts such as the Second World War and the Falklands/Malvinas dispute of 1982 can be said to fit this type of explanation. Such an interpretation has been intellectually supported by the development of the notion of structural violence, which is said to exist 'when economic and social conditions are such that people die or suffer as a consequence of the unequal distribution of resources, not as a result of physical violence' (see Tickner, 1994, p. 43; also Dunn, 1978, pp. 267–9).

Pausing for a moment in this historical development of PS, it should be easy to see that peace was subjected to a radical reconsideration; that the concern with inter-state war gave way in certain quarters to a concern with marginalized and oppressed groups and a much broader agenda. In retrospect, it therefore seems all the more remarkable that within IR as a whole, security remained the preserve of strategic studies so that fifteen years later Buzan could make his claims about what a poorly developed concept it was and that twenty or so years later IR itself should finally be subject to radical critiques which seek to put silenced voices at the centre of analysis. However, IR has been the most entrenched of disciplines and the defence of realism and neorealism, as well as security studies is not suprising (see Walt, 1991). This is not to suggest, however, that PS has simply travelled a road sooner than IR; recent epistemological challenges in IR stem from different causes than the PS debates of the 1960s, but it is simply to say that a greater awareness of the implications of work in PS *could* have greatly influenced IR.

Returning then to PS, David Dunn has suggested that there exists, in effect and at the level of analysis, a peace continuum with minimalist (negative) definitions at one end and maximalist (positive) ones at the other. The minimalist is concerned with the duration and observable causes of violent conflict and the reasons for its escalation, whilst the maximalists are involved in a much more *explicitly* normative enterprise and want to address issues of social injustice and the structural violence which causes it. One is tempted, though there would be problems with such an idea (as the previous chapters should suggest), to talk of a similar continuum in IR security studies today, in which a maximalist position would be a broader security agenda more clearly relevant to the world's poorer people. Though in both IR and PS Dunn's linear image is inadequate given current complexities, it is not an unreasonable way to make some sense of this complexity.

In terms of the initial motivations or *raison d'être* of PS, particularly pacifism as a virtue, the idea of this continuum presents some interesting ethical problems. If social justice requires structural changes, might those changes not need physical violence to bring them about? Advocating violence to achieve peace seems a long way from the origins of PS.[3] However, this is all part of a hugely diversifying agenda in IR in general, such as the legitimacy of wars of national liberation, which has not eluded the PS sub-field. In these times of *post*-Cold War, *post*modernism and *post*-just about everything else, PS is a remarkably broad area of enquiry. In order that IR does not forget its sub-field in forging a wider security studies agenda, the following section looks at (post)modern PS and at what is going on within it.

Modern Peace Studies

Despite the positive noises about how PS could have made a more pronounced contribution to IR there are at least two caveats. First, in many respects, PS continues along the track it started and has been less than radical. George Lopez argues that in the post-Cold War 'reconceptualization has been minimal compared to the magnitude of change' (1994, p. 3). The *Journal of Conflict Resolution*, for instance, has recently centred on traditionally focused articles on efforts to instil peace in violence-affected regions such as the Middle East and Northern Ireland. As a further example, Tickner argues that 'peace studies rarely investigates how women are differently affected by war [and/or] structural violence' (1994, p. 43). However, in some other respects PS can still be said to resemble the rapidly diversifying discipline of IR to which it is related and in all sorts of ways its agenda has widened and now includes, though this list is not exhaustive, environment, ethnicity, psychology, gender and law.

This brings us to the second caveat, offered by Lawler, that the PS research agenda is a black hole, that the sub-field has become blurred and unwieldy. Of course such breadth need not necessarily lead us to conclude that PS has nothing relevant to contribute to the security debate. What we would say is that Lawler's contention that 'the failure to establish a distinctive focus for peace research arises from an insufficient examination of the normative assumptions of peace research and the concomitant failure to theorise the critical and constructive functions of peace research [and that] as a consequence, peace research is replete with unfulfilled aspirations' (1990, p. 129) is worth thinking about; that a narrower focus, surrounding conceptions of what it means to be secure, 'while retaining the critical essence which motivated or inspired peace researchers in the first place' (p. 111) could be a profitable way forward both for PS and IR. However, Lawler's contention that 'greater precision in delineating the province of peace research would...improve its intellectual and practical worth' (p. 129) sounds as if it could be used as a rallying cry for a return to PS' sterile conservatism of the 1950s.

This section now seeks to outline the nature and extent of today's PS, and how it is changing, and does so for two reasons; the first is to demonstrate the relevance of PS to what might broadly be termed the 'third world', whilst the second is to remind ourselves of the closeness, in many ways, between peace and security and to hope that IR scholars maintain an awareness of the importance of this sub-field.[4] In the 1960s IR seemed so engrossed in its own methodological debates, assumed at the time to be of vital importance (see Vasquez, 1979), that it failed to pick up on various currents in PS which may well have enriched the discipline of IR. This is not to say that IR's current debates (its epistemological wrangles) do not have huge significance; simply that we ask that inputs from PS are not neglected a second time, despite the reservations about PS that we offered above.

Despite the 'positive peace' side of PS it is undoubtedly the case that focusing on large-scale political and social violence, particularly frequency and intensity of (especially great power) war, has long constituted the orthodoxy of the approach. In both Europe and the United States the 1970s and 1980s saw PS dominated by discussion of the nuclear arms race. However, as with IR more generally, the ending of the Cold War has allowed questions to be posed regarding new ways in which people are dying from political and social violence, given that civilians now constitute the majority of war casualties.[5] Thus, although it is most certainly true that 'the combination of genocide, gross violations of human rights, and bloody internal civil and ethnic violence has wreaked more havoc on the world scene than has organized warfare', it is only with the ending of the Cold War that PS has really entirely recognized the fact, especially in the United States (see Lopez, 1994, p. 6).

We can safely say that PS does not share the view that 'at the dawn of the twenty-first century, humanity has arrived at the "end of history" and a new world order of peace, justice, and security'. As mentioned above, PS has a whole range of concerns which it has added to its agenda, including gender and environmental issues. Significantly, in the context of this book, PS also seems to have woken up to concerns of the third world, where the concept of structural violence has multiple significances; 'it is in the so-called "Third World"... that political violence is most advanced and routinized. Gun-wielding youth, death squads, disappearances, torture, and pervasive human rights violations constitute the way of life in many parts of the impoverished "south". Massive dumping of arms by superpowers during the Cold War has been followed by political destabilisation at the end of the Cold War' (Bandarage, 1994, p. 29).[6]

Here there are two crucial ideas or themes. The first concerns the way third world societies have become militarized and the consequences thereof, and the second theme, which is connected, is concerned with poverty as structural violence. The first is clearly a result of Cold War priorities in which the superpower protagonists bought (that is, paid for) themselves an era of unprecedented Cold War peace at the price of 'hot (proxy) wars' and suffering and insecurity throughout the third world. Here 'insecurity' is used in a generalized way since it could apply to non-traditional agendas (both broader and deeper), newer understandings and the traditional military sphere and the notion of insecurity spirals (see Jervis, 1976). This is very much connected with the second issue of poverty as structural violence; the gifts of arms were accompanied by loans to buy more arms and frequently stimulated self-perpetuating and spiralling expenditures by states themselves such that 'a large percentage of the Third World debt today represents monies borrowed to purchase arms from the industrialized world' (Bandarage, 1994, p. 31). However, poverty as a structural problem has longer roots, stemming back to the transformation of subsistence economies into commodity production for export and a system of unequal trade set in motion by imperialism (see Chapter 1). As Eduardo Galeano points out, under this system of so-called *comparative advantage* some countries specialize in winning and others in losing (1974, p. 4). One can win by exporting expensive manufactured goods, including military equipment, and one loses by having one's natural resources cheaply extracted; this is not a question of choice.

In adopting such concerns, PS is very close to mirroring developments in IR, although it comes from different directions. In arguing for attention to be paid to PS, this issue of background is crucial. Whilst IR has built up its own body of 'knowledge', a 'literature' constantly referred to, to be learnt by students new to the discipline, PS has always been more self-consciously multi-disciplinary, bringing in contributions from relevant social theory. Thus

Galtung's highly significant contributions are those of a sociologist (Galtung, 1971). When PS first took on the attributes of a formal 'subject' or area at the Stanford University Center for Advanced Study in the Behavioral Sciences (1954–55), those who helped to launch PS in the United States were an economist, a mathematical biologist, a political scientist, a social psychologist, and an anthropologist – all were to play seminal role(s) in the development of peace studies (Dunn, 1978, p. 262).

Though we have already covered feminism in a previous chapter, it is important to note the contribution that gender issues are making to PS – asking not to be tacked on to Peace Studies courses and degrees but to play a fundamental role in shaping attitudes to issues of war and violence. As in IR's corpus of literature, gender neutrality has similarly been assumed in PS. However, in 'seeking a more robust definition of peace as freedom from all sources of oppression', feminists hope that gender analysis and feminist perspectives will prove their worth as part of PS subject matter; the linkages to IR and security should be readily apparent (Tickner, 1994, p. 44; see also Tickner, 1995). There are a number of important reasons for incorporating a gender analysis into PS. In the first instance there is a strong association between masculinity and soldiering in which in order to be a soldier one must first be a 'man'. Second, in the world of strategic planning, language is heavily masculine; whilst this may not determine national security policy it is likely to limit options considered and shape expectations (see also Chapter 3).

The argument here is not that PS has somehow been the field, approach or discipline that IR might have been had it not clung to the old certainties and handed-down truths. Neither is the argument that we can easily suggest how PS might inform the security debate. It does not even suggest that PS has avoided some of the mistakes, such as gender 'neutrality', that IR has done. It is simply to suggest that, even *within* IR (in what has after all been regarded as a sub-field, that is, PS), much seems to have been missed which could have illuminated the security debate, or at the very least caused it to happen earlier, as the historical purview of this chapter has sought to demonstrate. Accordingly, and the epistemological debates alluded to in Chapter 3 should make this clear, IR must be much more open and flexible in its consideration of the international.

Political Geography

In some institutions, Political Geography (PG) is a part of a broadly defined International Studies and its practitioners consider themselves very much a part of an IR-type discipline. Nonetheless, there are differences in approach and foundational literatures between the two such that they are kept apart; degree courses can be very separate and little engagement takes place. We argue here that whilst this separation may have good reasons, IR and PG have much to benefit from cross-fertilization.

Basically, as IR looks to re-evaluate a core term, it can become of more interest to political geographers interested in such issues as health, gender and migration. Similarly, for political geographers, as the term 'third world' comes under scrutiny so do other metageographical constructs which have *naturally* shaped the world for scholars of both IR and PG alike (Lewis and Wigen, 1997). The point here, as it relates to either 'security' or the 'third world', is not intended to be unduly sophisticated or dwelt upon. It is simply to suggest that students of IR, at any level, should keep an eye on developments in PG; that IR's isolation should end.

Conclusions

In order to make clear why and how the remaining chapters are relevant and how they hang together, it is useful at this point to recapitulate explicitly on what has been attempted thus far. Initially, this book dealt with the introductory and fundamental ideas of changing agendas, re-definition and new thinking. It looked at the history of security as a concept (Introduction) and at the well-known, but equally shifting notion of the third world (Chapter 1) in order to provide the background for further discussion. The subsequent four chapters (2 to 5) have sought to put some meat on these bones as it were, and have discussed some different theoretical tools for dealing with once rigid meta-concepts that have looked increasingly 'woolly'. This has been attempted not by coming up with our own re-definitions but by suggesting to the reader a variety of ways of coming to terms with increasing complexity.

We started in Chapter 2 within disciplinary IR itself and power politics' long-unchallenged assumptions, looking at how this realist tradition has been adapted in the work of some authors so as to incorporate a broader conception of security, in the form of various neorealist analyses. We then considered how this has seen a concept develop with arguably greater relevance to the states, if not the peoples, of the third world. Such work has provided a subtle defence of orthodoxy by securitizing issues only as they relate to states, but at the same time has recognized the geographical and issue boundedness of IR.

Moving on to more contemporary debates within IR scholarship, Chapter 3 on critical theory, postmodernism and feminist theorizing noted how the whole realist enterprise has finally been seriously undermined within the discipline by various poststructuralist approaches. These approaches have sought to give voices to the marginalized, and whilst we cannot say that they have led to a new definition of security, this has not been their aim. What they have worked towards are new ways of thinking which ensure that a voice is given to those who have most experienced *insecurity*. It is in this sense that they are of crucial relevance to the third world, which constitutes the poor and marginalized,[7] however we choose to define it.

Moving away from developments strictly within IR, Chapter 4 deals with environmental thought. The idea of environmental security can be bandied around in policy discourse as if it were self-evident. However, the chapter is included not because there is any widespread agreement on such an idea, since there is not, but for two important reasons. First, in the empirical realm, because in the current global economy environmental threats are seeming to increase and a global environmental agenda has emerged, from the possibility of 'water wars' in the Middle East, to the hole in the ozone layer and the threats of rising sea-levels and nuclear accidents. Second, because the huge diversity of environmental or ecological philosophies provides a number of ways into thinking about security in the third world. What Chapter 4 sought to do was show that beyond and behind debates on this subject which consider environmental diplomacy, the relative role of poorer and richer countries as well as non-governmental organizations (NGOs), scientists and so on in environmental protection, there is actually a whole body of green political theory envisaging radically restructured societies which would imply radical differences in the understanding of what it means to be secure. The 'shallow' responses currently proposed are challenged by currently hidden 'deep' perspectives which envisage a different type of security for individuals and communities throughout the world.

Peace and security would not seem very far apart in many people's common-sense list of terms. However, whilst peace research/studies worked hard to develop, or at least debate, the meaning of peace, IR seemed content to leave security as an uncontested bastion of Strategic Studies and to work within a certain prescribed set of truths and literatures.[8] In this chapter on PS we have sought to emphasize the developments which have taken place within this sub-field of IR and the potential importance they could have had, and may still have, in an expanded peace and security studies of the future. The short section on PG attempted to highlight the potential for cross-fertilization between various disciplines, warning IR to be less reticent in engaging with the work of scholars in related fields but perhaps using unfamiliar terms or literatures.

Accordingly, to this point, we have looked at various aspects of the security debate and have argued that in notable ways, even within the main (male) stream, it has acquired considerably more relevance in the context of what has been known as the third world; we have also highlighted some of the problems with this term and fundamentally suggested that within and outside disciplinary IR there are a whole range of tools which can help us to think about the related problematics of changing security agendas and the third world.

What we hope to do from this point onwards is to suggest the ways in which we have attempted to understand the idea of 'changing security agendas and the third world'. We hope to show how the tools we have suggested, as well as the need for IR to engage more broadly in terms of its influences, can be used when thinking about security and the third world. We will show that in practical contexts and in theoretical terms (especially concerning ontological and epistemological questions which surround the security concept/debate in IR), the shifting definitions and ways of thinking suggested by this book can actually be applied. It is worth stressing again that this does not imply a logical end-point to an argument, but more a demonstration of 'applied IR', and that in our conclusions we will try to draw out a range of themes which might receive further attention.

Thus Chapter 6 outlines research into the historical separation of the security and development discourses and suggests how an understanding of this separation could make a valuable contribution to the analysis of security in the future. We look at the congruent theoretical investments of both realist and modernization theory and argue that in breaking down historical barriers security and development can be very different. Informed by fieldwork in Vietnam and Laos we advance arguments surrounding community security and empowerment in concrete contexts.

Following this, we look at *sustainable* development in Chapter 7; this has frequently been either dismissed as being little more than an extension of the development discourse or embraced as the needed response to the consequences of modernity and processes of globalization. We look at the roots of sustainable development (in Northern environmentalism as much as the development discourse) and at critiques of the concept, as well as the potential for its mediation within local contexts, in order to assess the possibility that it might contribute to a genuinely more secure ecological future. The chapter seeks to emphasize that sustainable development is very much what is made of it rather than the miracle cure which will finally make an egalitarian success of the free market. Bolivia, which had the world's first Ministry of Sustainable Development and Environment (Ministerio de Desarrollo Sostenible y Medio Ambiente; MDSMA), provides the practical context in which to look at sustainable development.

Notes

1. Perhaps what Lawler (1990) calls a 'disdain for...theoretical reflection' is what has held PS back, 'theoretical reflection' being exactly what Buzan (1983, 1991) was aiming at.
2. In our own university, for instance, a course on IR theory recently removed the lecture on peace research from its programme.
3. Violence is clearly an idea that needs exploration despite its common-sense meaning (see Campbell and Dillon, 1993).
4. It is undoubtedly the case that there are fundamental differences between 'peace' in PS and 'security' within Strategic Studies. However, looking at their 'common-sense' opposites of violence and insecurity gives a clearer idea of how potentially close the two terms are.
5. An exact figure is not offered here since difficulties may arise from differences between terms (for example, war and conflict). Within the same book, Lopez suggests that civilian casualties of war are 'nearly 75 percent' compared to less than 50 per cent in the 1950s (1994, p. 6) whilst Tickner uses different data, estimating that 'up to 90 percent of total casualties in conflicts since 1945 have been civilians' (1994, p.47).
6. Bandarage uses double quotation marks around "Third World" for the following reason: 'The term *Third World* is pejorative. In the absence of a "Second World" it has even less meaning. Still other alternative terms such as *developing world, the South* and so on do not capture the exploitative nature of the relations between the West and the neocolonial nations of Asia, Africa, and Latin America. Hence the term *Third World* is retained in this article' (1994, p. 29).
7. This relates directly to the original French understanding of *Tiers État* (see Chapter 1).
8. The word 'content' might imply that IR was happy not to change the situation; this should be interpreted as a lack of awareness that change was even possible.

References

Bandarage, A. (1994) 'Global peace and security in the post-Cold War era: a "third world" perspective'. In Klare, M. (ed.) *Peace and World Security Studies*. Boulder, CO: Lynne Rienner, pp. 29–42.

Buzan. B. (1983) *People, States and Fear: The National Security Problem in International Relations*, 1st edition. Brighton: Wheatsheaf.

Buzan, B. (1991) *People, States and Fear: An Agenda for International Security Studies in the Post Cold War Era*, 2nd edition. Hemel Hempstead: Harvester Wheatsheaf.

Campbell, D. and Dillon, M. (eds) (1993) *The Political Subject of Violence*. Manchester: Manchester University Press.

Deudney, D. (1991) 'Environment and security: muddled thinking', *Bulletin of Atomic Scientists*, 47 (3), 22–8.

Deutsch, K. (1978) *The Analysis of International Relations*, 2nd edition. Englewood Cliffs, NJ: Prentice Hall.

Dunn, D. 'Peace research'. In Taylor, T. (ed.) (1978) *Approaches and Theory in International Relations*. London: Longmans, pp. 257–79.

Galeano, E. (1974) *The Open Veins of Latin America: Five Centuries of the Pillage of a Continent*. New York: Monthly Review Press.

Galtung, J. (1971) 'A structural theory of imperialism', *Journal of Peace Research*, 13 (2), 81–117.

Galtung, J. (1975–80) *Essays in Peace Research (Volumes One to Five)*. Copenhagen: Christian Ejlers.

Jervis, R. (1976) *Perception and Misperception in World Politics*. Princeton: Princeton University Press.

Lawler, P. (1990) 'New directions in peace research'. In Emy H. and Linklater, A. (eds) *Australian Perspectives in International Relations*. Sydney: Allen and Unwin, pp. 109–31.

Lewis, M.W. and Wigen, K.E. (1997) *The Myth of Continents: A Critique of Metageography*. Berkeley, CA: University of California Press.

Lopez, G. (1994) 'Changes to curriculum development in the post-Cold War era'. In Klare, M. (ed.) *Peace and World Security Studies*. Boulder, CO: Lynne Rienner, pp. 3–13.

Morgenthau, H. (1978) *Politics among Nations: The Struggle for Power and Peace*, 5th edition. New York: Alfred Knopf.

Richardson, L.F. (1960) *Statistics of Deadly Quarrels*. Chicago: Quadrangle.

Shaw, M. (1993) 'There is no such thing as society: beyond individualism and statism in international security studies', *Review of International Studies*, 19 (2), 159–76.

Smith, M.J. (1986) *Realist Thought: From Weber to Kissinger*. Baton Rouge, LA: University of Louisiana Press.

Tickner, J.A. (1994) 'Feminist perspectives on peace and world security in the post-Cold War era'. In Klare, M. (ed.) *Peace and World Security Studies*. Boulder, CO: Lynne Rienner, pp. 43–54.

Tickner, J.A. (1995) 'Re-visioning security'. In Booth, K. and Smith, S. (eds) *International Relations Theory Today*. Cambridge: Cambridge University Press, pp. 175–97.

Vasquez, J. (1979) 'Colouring it Morgenthau', *Review of International Studies*, 5 (3), 210–18.

Walt, S. (1991) 'The renaissance of security studies', *International Studies Quarterly*, 35 (2), 211–35.

Wright, Q. (1942) *A Study of War*. Chicago: Chicago University Press.

6

Security and Development: Exploring Conceptual and Practical Linkages

One of the failures of traditional security discourses in the contemporary international environment has been an inability to incorporate how people mediate, negotiate and participate in coping strategies to reduce the insecurities faced in day-to-day life. It is well documented that the majority of people in the third world experience hunger, land loss and malnutrition, as well as poor access to education and health services. While much progress has been made in the postwar era in terms of life expectancy, education, health, sanitation, food and nutrition and the status of women, development indicators illustrate continuing human degradation; average life expectancy in the third world remains twelve years shorter than in the first world, nearly three million children die each year from immunizable diseases, three billion people still live without adequate sanitation and maternal mortality rates in the third world are 122 times those in the first world (United Nations Development Programme (UNDP) Report in Allen and Thomas, 1993, p. 237).

In the post-Cold War era, as international political alignments restructured after the fall of communism, and other pressures (such as environmental degradation and international migration) emerged, the framework of traditional security seems unable to cope. This chapter sets out to explore how the debate about security can be linked in theoretical and practical ways to issues which have been largely the domain of Development Studies (DS). The rise of neoliberal development thinking to a position of dominance within DS, resulted, in some ways, in the failure of the discipline to impact positively in discussion about the marginalization of the poor in political, social and economical terms.

Indeed, the so-called 'impasse' in development theory in the 1980s was a reflection of the failure of development *policy* to substantially improve living conditions in the third world.[1] Often called the 'lost decade', the 1980s saw a decline in most social indicators through policies of structural adjustment and economic austerity programmes.

This chapter attempts to make the concept of security more relevant to the third world in International Relations (IR), but also to explore how security as an analytical tool can be more relevant to those people who are marginalized and poor in society. It has two main aims. The first is to survey key reasons why the traditional security debate within IR did not incorporate social problems, such as poverty, which existed predominantly in the third world. It builds upon the critique of realism and neorealism presented in Chapter 3 to consider the implications of their theoretical bias for a more people-orientated version of security. By investigating the dilemmas around contemporary security studies we can begin to think about 'global politics in ways that are not reduced to the territorial and ethnocentric discourses of (national) security' (Dalby, 1997, p. 25). It also asks how the opening of the security debate to incorporate problems central to the third world has been possible.

Moving from critique, the second aim of the chapter is more productive. It develops the framework for what we call a micro-security approach. At a practical level, this approach makes the connections between community development and security, noting how development strategies for increased income security, food security, educational opportunities and access to services can be at the same time tied to individual and community coping strategies. These have been issues foreign to IR but present in the DS literature on participatory development approaches, resistance and coping mechanisms, in conjunction with non-governmental organizations (NGOs) and other development agencies. A micro-security approach which focuses on life at the local level can illustrate not only the redundancy of Cold War, traditional security approaches for third world people, but also how autonomous and indigenous strategies of development are able to increase physical survival and conditions of living. This approach must be said to be the basic premise of security.[2] The exploration of a micro-security approach forms part of a number of possible themes for further research in security studies. It occupies and opens up a critical and normative space in which issues of development and their interaction and connection with security interests can take place.

The Development Discourse in International Relations

It would be incorrect to say that IR as a discipline totally marginalized the third world from its analysis. However, as argued in Chapters 1 and 2, the third world's inclusion was predominantly in terms of how particular states were positioned *vis-à-vis* the political division between the former Soviet Union and the United States, and their importance to perceived national security interests of the superpowers or their allies. More recently, however, the discipline has begun to engage with the third world as a category of states and with issues particularly pertinent to them in a more critical and meaningful way. The first trend has been IR's engagement with the marginalization of poverty from the discipline. Part of this line of analysis has been to trace how the dominant school of realist thought incorporated a particular and implicit understanding of development into the discipline – one which coincided with assumptions of realist theory and underpinned many foreign policy concerns and goals of the United States. These concerns fed into the discipline of IR to establish a constant exchange between the academy and government around US priorities in the foreign policy arena.[3] Here we explore the first theme before moving on to the second: the development of critical security studies.

At this point it is important to understand the implication of modernization ideals, firstly in how IR assigned primacy to the state, rising from the development of the modern state system, and secondly how the modern state system became the vehicle and political form of capitalist development. Saurin argues that IR's adoption of a particular ideological narrative or 'official transcript' of development within its discourse, expressed in modernization ideals of the *primacy* of economic growth and unilinear progress, served to exclude analysis of subordinated people by allocating the state agency in historical change (1996, pp. 666–7). IR as a discipline subscribed to aspirations and presumptions of the modernist project that 'the world could be made a better place and, crucially, political-economic programmes devised through systematic (and violent) abstraction would guarantee these improvements' (p. 664). There are clear similarities between the respective philosophical bases of IR and DS. With antecedents in post-enlightenment thinking, both liberal IR and development theories embody the *modern* promise of overcoming natural determination: (international) politics as an escape from a Hobbesian state of nature; development as a triumph over a state of savagery (Pasha, 1996, p. 640).

The role the state adopted in the universal practice of development indicators like gross domestic product (GDP) masked the insecurity of poverty and the particular local and global social relations which constituted them. Pasha argues that the process of globalization is implicated in this process firstly through the subversion of public policy by international development organizations with a neoliberal agenda and secondly by uncurtailed domestic and international capital markets. 'This subversion, or global political-economic reconstruction, has, according to the neo-liberal orthodoxy, ensured that production, allocation, and distribution of resources is to be determined principally by the "market" and not by the "state"' (Saurin, 1996, p. 673). Through this process, a 'naturalization of poverty' through 'naturalization of the market' constructs poverty as inevitable and irremovable; 'thus conceived, state attempts to regulate or ameliorate the condition of poverty are reconstructed as futile obstacles to progress' (Saurin, 1996, p. 673). Development policy and planning in this scenario have firmly shifted from being state led to a function of the market driven by international capital.

It has been argued that the raw material for the study of international relations remains self-serving representations of the state, and that the way in which the state portrays forced social change is favourable to itself and at the same time suppresses the possibility of alternative ways of understanding change (Saurin, 1996, pp. 658–9). This 'neutralization of criticism' in orthodox IR discourse renders the lives and actions of the poor and powerless invisible in analysis. This concern for the denial of agency to the poor and powerless within IR discourse leads Saurin to point out that alternative histories and explanations of social change must be acknowledged in and of themselves and not merely because 'they are implicated in the dominant history' but for their own autonomous history (p. 660).

The discussion of poverty, destitution and inequality in IR has often been subordinate to debates over economic reform according to the rhetoric of neoliberal globalization (Pasha, 1996, p. 635). As argued above, both IR and DS shared a common belief in creating a better world. Liberal IR theorists sought to attain this through political organization of the state while developmentalists sought to create it through acquisition of wealth, although one can see the connections through the state as the political form of capitalism. Accordingly, IR has engaged in a discourse based on *space* (state territory and sovereignty) concerned with the *political* organization of space; DS has engaged in a discourse around *time* (movement from one stage of growth to another, backward to modern, primitive to civilized) concerned with the *economic* transition to the modern (Pasha, 1996, pp. 640–1). In both disciplines, however, the third world is considered closer to nature or a natural state or, put another way, 'the cultural and relational attributes of the "poor" are seen mainly as biological, not as a social state or condition' (p. 640). The poor have been denied a sense of agency through the lack of recognition of their history and action, and through the way that anarchy was used in IR to 'naturalize' world order, so that human action and agency were lost in the construction of 'International Society'.[4]

On a practical level, the state may be undergoing a restructuring of its role in poverty alleviation in the contemporary global political economy, where poverty, destitution or inequality, obscured by neoliberal globalization rhetoric, is subordinate to issues of economic reform. A significant consequence of the state's withdrawal as the primary agent in poverty alleviation has been the burden being placed increasingly on civil society, including (NGOs):

> Curiously, the neo-liberal penchant for promoting a market-based order, private capital, and non-state agents in place of social planning, public spending, and the role of a development state coincides with the liberal advocacy of civil society and global civil society (GCS) as the new social spaces for overcoming the conceit of statist thinking in politics as well as development. (Pasha, 1996, p. 639)[5]

The neoliberal agenda of economic globalization also has implications for the role of non-state actors in the third world. Pasha argues that neoliberal economic agendas overlap with global civil society discourse to mount an attack on the third world state; 'enfeebled by internal tensions and pressured to globalise, the state becomes incapable of denying an augmented role to non-state actors', namely NGOs amongst others (Pasha, 1996, p. 645). The increasing role for NGOs as new providers of social security nets as the state withdraws neither questions the structural causes of global inequality nor reflexively locates the structural location and function of non-state actors in the global political economy.

The lack of attention to the poor and issues close to them (*defined* by them) can also be seen to be excluded from IR analysis through the discipline's epistemological basis – the rationalist, self-interested logic of neoliberal economic theory. This is because much action, experience and knowledge of poor people lies outside the theoretical and empirical umbrella of IR the discipline, which is founded on a certain construction of power which objectifies human life through what is considered to be rational behaviour. It has been in this way that poor people's actions have become 'mysterious'; even when given visibility, validity is not extended to their experiences and needs. Through the imposition of universal categories drawn from quite specific historical, political and economic contexts, through a narrow account of human behaviour and through a concept of power based on resources, the poor and their needs have been marginalized (Tooze and Murphy, 1996, pp. 688–9).

In summary, the critical theme of the writers referred to in this section has been to question and offer epistemological and practical explanations for the marginalization of poverty, in particular, from IR. In addition, they develop in different ways an overtly normative argument for greater consideration of poverty as a political problem and how the process and shifts in the international economic and political environment relate to 'development' as praxis.

A More Critical Security Studies

A second trend in IR's movement towards engaging with the third world and problems particular to it has been the development of critical security studies and the broadened concept of security which has resulted. This trend has developed alongside the acknowledgement of the marginalization of poverty within the discipline, as discussed above. Key to this debate has been how poverty alleviation has been linked to shifts occurring in the state's role in the global political economy. The state's diminishing role in poverty alleviation as a primary goal are positioned within a wider debate about the state in international and domestic economic policy (Kothari, 1993; Pasha, 1996). Influenced by neoliberal economic policies, the state has allegedly shifted from being the main actor and vehicle in poverty alleviation to merely the political structure for the effective operation of capitalism. Debates about the shifting and relative power of the state in the context of globalization are also an important impetus for the development of critical security studies. Indeed, as Dalby argues,

> the dilemma of academic security discourse after the Cold War is precisely that its conceptual infrastructure has long outlived any usefulness it might have once had and has mutated into a number of discourses that operate to maintain the unjust political order of developed

and underdeveloped and over-consumption in the developed world at the expense of degradation of the global environment. (1997, pp. 4–5)

It is very helpful to identify and distinguish between these 'mutated discourses'. Firstly, it is because the expansion and reformulations of security have presented security studies and the contemporary discipline of IR with destabilizing questions. Secondly, it is because through some of these mutating discourses that other trends like an increased interest in poverty and problems of the third world have found discursive space in IR within the new critical security family. One destabilizing factor is how new ways of understanding security introduce and represent a number of political problems which have neither traditionally had space in IR nor been seen as politically problematic. The way in which the discipline then addresses the incorporation of new political agendas will be significant.[6]

How then has critical security studies developed and why has this been important for the need to integrate issues of poverty, inequality and basic human needs into IR? The exploration of how security should be reformulated to accommodate new circumstances in the post-Cold War era has been the conceptual and practical problem behind both questions. Critical security studies evolved from the recognition that new issues such as the restructuring of the nation-state in the global political economy, in response to changes in geopolitical environment, increasing global environmental degradation and widespread poverty and inequality, could not be accommodated within narrow confines of Cold War national-security discourse.

Responses within the academy to the inadequacy of national security discourses have taken a number of forms. Efforts to broaden the remit of security included discussion of how to include such areas as economic security, environmental security, societal insecurities, drugs and human rights into a wider security umbrella (Dalby, 1997, p. 6). Feminists such as Cynthia Enloe (1989, 1993), Ann Tickner (1992) and Christine Sylvester (1994) have tried to show how the national security discourse served to marginalize and silence women from decision-making roles in relation to foreign policy, and thus its limited utility as a political strategy to address structural inequality and environmental degradation, both of which have a negative disproportionate effect on women in society. Booth, in his influential 1991 article, did an about-turn on his former realist self to suggest that security should be linked to emancipatory goals where 'security means the absence of threats' and emancipation 'is the freeing of people (as individuals and groups) from those physical and human constraints which stop them carrying out what they would freely choose to do' (p. 319). Security and emancipation then, he argued, are 'two sides of the same coin [where] emancipation, *not power or order* [emphasis added], produces true security' (p. 319).[7]

The shift from state security to focus on societal security, exemplified by the work of the Copenhagen school (Wæver *et al.*, 1989; Buzan *et al.*, 1990; Wæver *et al.*, 1993; Buzan, Wæver and De Wilde, 1997), has been another trend which attempts to analyse how internal societal factors (migration, population, culture and so on) enrich our understanding of the complexity of security factors within the modern state without moving fundamentally from a state-centric framework.

A key contradiction to be addressed in the development of new approaches and reformulations of security is how security is linked to the need for major political change, which, contrary to its role in traditional realist and neorealist frameworks, involves a subversive political position (Dalby, 1997, pp. 4–5). The discourse of national security, informed by neorealist theory, represented the maintenance of US dominance of world politics as continuity and stability. Therefore the addition of an overtly political role for security, in an albeit alternative version, understandably represents political blurring of conceptual clarity bemoaned by the orthodoxy (see Ayoob, 1995, 1997).

One of the new 'mutant' security discourses, human security, which relates security to conditions of existence and immediate vulnerability, is not logically connected to the conventional understanding of security. Linking the individual as referent object of security with development issues addressing conditions of existence might seem logical in its own right; however, within the Cold War version of national security, where the state provides citizens the necessary requirements of being secure, it has little relevance. To couple security with inherently political questions of poverty and inequality and the structural (political and economic) causes is to link security with a project diametrically opposed to the neorealist formulation. As Dalby points out, these new readings of the security discourse, in addition to the formulation of a security politics, destabilize and contest the term itself (1997, p. 6). While in one sense critical security studies has created space for greater inclusion of third world issues, it has posed fundamental ethical and epistemological questions of the discipline's role as agent and participant in social activism and change.

Can some explanations be found in deconstructing the epistemological and political implications of neorealism's positivist assumptions? Simon Dalby sees this as a central task. Through these assumptions, neorealism's methodology suggested that 'most, if not all, things are both knowable and hence predictable through the application of social scientific methods and [that] reasoning is intimately related to the formulations of security as the *management and control of risks and threats* [emphasis added]' (1997, p. 24). Clearly, one can not pre-empt all possible threats, but the emphasis in neorealism on the possibility for management and control of certain types of threats implies that political and military interventions offer the possibility of managing international politics (*ibid.*).

The definition of the political in neorealism, linked both to the ontological status of the state and to the geopolitical or territorial orders (internal to the discipline) which were constructed by the state system, has found difficulty in offering useful analytical tools with which to interpret post-Cold War conditions. Dalby argues that the narrow and constraining definition of politics is at its most exposed when conceptualizing politics 'in such terms as the *local* and the *global*, terms that often seem to have more resonance with political experience than do the geopolitical rituals of statecraft' (1997, p. 20). He argues that, combined with the legitimation of political and military intervention, security in this framework functions to normalize and extirpate difference, further justifying violence as appropriate political practice and excluding fuller exploration of complexity and difference in social systems (*ibid.*). The difficulty within neorealism, methodologically and politically, to conceptualize relationships between the local and the global is a key reason for the marginalization of poverty from its analysis. Poverty as a problem was situated in the internal domain of individual sovereign states, and it was one which bore no major significance to the tools at the disposal of neorealist foreign policy. Crucially, it is in the complexity and diversity of these relations between the local and global which have made the reconceptualization of security both vitally needed and extremely difficult. The inappropriateness of traditional security discourses to accommodate new issues on the post-Cold War security agenda has been at the same time an important impetus for the restructuring of IR.

Changing the Gaze: A View from the Third World

While many of the catalysts for this reformulation of security studies emanated from the Western academy in the wake of the post-Cold War era, the insecurities suffered by the third world during the Cold War remain unchanged. It would be incorrect to think that the opening up of the security discourse to include issues more relevant to the third world has changed material conditions which were, and continue to be, major threats to state, societal, community and individual security. Indeed, Acharya argues that the concentration in traditional security discourse on an ethnocentric nation state system, which focuses primarily on the responses and interests of Western governments and societies to war (especially the United States), involved the concurrent exclusions of the issues and experiences of the other major part of international state system – the third world. Being other unto the West, however, resulted in third world issues and experiences 'not fully incorporated into the discourse of security studies' (1997, p. 300).

The lived experience of third world states posed a challenge, even in the Cold War era, to the dominant understanding of security. The emergence of the third world, with its diversity of external and internal security threats, challenged the security discourse in three ways: 'its focus on the intra-state level as the point of origin of security threats; its exclusion of non-military phenomena from the security studies agenda; and its belief in the global balance of power as the legitimate and effective instrument in international order' (Acharya, 1997, p. 301). As discussed previously in the book and in the above section, neorealist discourse, and realist discourse before it, maintained its analysis at and above the level of the state. Whilst having the obvious effect of excluding sub-state factors from discussion, it also denied the possibility that the state *itself* could pose the major threat to its citizens, rather than being the provider of security constructed in the neorealist analysis. The exclusion of non-military factors from the security studies agenda was both a function of neorealism's epistemology and the methodology which followed; the preoccupation with the prevention of war between states did not form part of the national security agenda. The third factor, the role of the balance of power and anarchy as a structuring force in the international system, effectively removed third world states from playing an active part in its discourse, as balance of power politics relegated them to the sidelines merely to watch the proceedings of superpower rivalry or be victims of it. And on the individual and community level, the central role of anarchy within neorealist theory, its account of change through the *structure* of the state system, denied a significant role for agents to act below the state.

One of the arguments against broadening security as a concept has been the apprehension that security would lose its conceptual clarity and analytical worth (see Ayoob, 1997; Walt, 1991). However, upon examination of the threats which are considered in the broadening agenda — pollution, environmental degradation, poverty, resource scarcity and so on — these issues have always been more pertinent for the third world. Conditions of existence did not form part of the national security agenda of third world countries, yet their connection between the balance of conflict and order was, unlike in the first world, present, such as in social unrest due to food shortages. It is the way in which non-military and societal security issues are of greater practical, political, economic and institutional concern to national security that makes the traditional security discourse more defunct for the third world under contemporary conditions. This is not to suggest that non-military and societal threats should not be considered in their own right, as we argue in the next section. It is rather that critical security studies attempts to highlight past inadequacies of national security discourse, 'with the third world serving as a central conceptual and empirical focus', to aid in understanding its future role in the international system (Acharya, 1997, p. 317).

Towards a Micro-Security Approach

Deconstructing the contemporary security discourse, its theoretical antecedents and current formation identifies the inapplicability of the traditional notion of security for many contemporary circumstances. The redundancy of Cold War security approaches to issues common to the third world requires further thought about what is involved with the exploration of multi-securities in a 'post-security' security framework. The need to develop ways to understand the complexity of security relationships between the state and its citizens must be prominent on the list of priorities. As discussed above, neorealism's difficulty in conceptualizing links between the local and the global is part of that complexity which requires further analysis. A micro-security approach, sketched out in this section, sets the agenda with these types of questions. Such an approach, which is based largely at the community level, accounts for and assigns importance to coping strategies and mechanisms, and resistance strategies, in which individuals, often as communities, participate. These processes are both in response to vulnerable living conditions and as a form of resisting pressures from changes in production conditions, government policy, globalization, environmental degradation and so on, which affect conditions of existence and community life in the third world.

Theoretically, then, considering security from the standpoint of communities and their role in action and mediation implies a greater role for agency than assigned within traditional security discourse, where the ontological status of the state in practice functioned as provider of security. Within this framework, individuals and communities were passive recipients of 'security' – the subjects – whereas the state was the object of analysis. Turning this opposition around redresses the lack of emphasis on the actions and decisions of communities, while providing a framework within which the complexities of local/global connections and state–individual–community relationships can be explored. It also forms part of the project to understand politics as about more than state-based territory, which realism and neorealism encouraged.

Neorealism's methodology is problematic for micro-security not because it assists formulations of security as management and control of risks and threats *per se*, but because risks and threats were largely to the state, in all its forms, and management and control of them was largely through militarized and/or state-sanctioned mechanisms. The fuller exploration of complexity and difference in social systems that Dalby hopes critical security studies will foster requires a methodological approach, or approaches, which make that possible, or at least plausible. Methods outside IR drawing from critical ethnography and DS, which are culturally sensitive and which allow focus on actors in the community, seem particularly useful tools to engage with micro-security issues in the third world. Some of the priorities and implications of these are outlined below before we move on to consider some practical contexts in which this approach might be applied.

Methodological Issues

Critical ethnographic (Ferguson, 1990; Pigg, 1992) and actor-orientated methodological approaches (Long, 1990) have a number of critical and productive uses for the study of indigenous security meaning in the third world. Ferguson, for example, uses a critical anthropological approach to look at the international development apparatus in a particular setting,

Lesotho in Africa. His method maintains that structures do not simply and rationally represent and express objective interests but that they are 'multi-layered, polyvalent, and often contradictory' (Ferguson, 1990, p. 17). The interests and investments of such structures 'can only operate through a complex set of social and cultural structures so deeply embedded and so ill-perceived that the outcome may be only a baroque and unrecognizable transformation of the original intention' (*ibid.*). Pigg's study similarly considers the introduction of development concepts into a Nepalese community, and concentrates on the construction of 'the village' as an effect of the development apparatus (Escobar, 1995, p. 48). Pigg considers how development 'alters the meaning of the village in Nepalese social imagination' and how 'in transforming both the terms in which social identities are cast and the symbols that mark social differences, development has effects that are cultural' (1992, pp. 491–2). This suggests that the development apparatus has important implications for a study of micro-security, including cultural and historical factors. Issues of identity and culture and how they relate to the ways and forms in which strategies are conducted to increase security within communities is an important task. In this sense, the methodology used to study specific local situations is helpful.

An actor-orientated approach (Long, 1990) considers the complex interactions between individuals, social groups and outside actors (for example, NGOs and state development bodies). Attempting to explain different responses to similar structural circumstances, it incorporates space for agency on the part of the actor. Such approaches assume that patterns of social organization are not imposed on individuals from above by structural logic but emerge through social interactions, negotiations and struggles. In this sense, decisions made within social frameworks are located within certain discourses and these discourses form part of the resources (knowledge) available to each social actor. Specific cultural contexts can therefore be incorporated in the analysis. An actor-orientated approach accounts for the agency of human actors while recognizing their connection to larger structures of meaning. Thus the role of microanalysis – the study of everyday experiences and strategies – is important from this perspective. Hannerz is one cultural theorist who has focused on the relationship between the first and the third world in global cultural interaction and who considers the strength of cultural resources which exist in 'everyday forms of life' at the community level. The significance for micro-security analysis is in how cultural resources assist the development and maintenance of coping and resistance strategies in response to changing conditions of vulnerability and sustainability of conditions of existence.

Hannerz explores two scenarios of globalization in relation to the cultural relationship between the third and the first world, or core and periphery: those of global homogenization and peripheral corruption. In the former, globalization theorists argue that homogenization occurs through cultural flows, driven by the market from the centre to the periphery, so that 'global culture' will be a version of contemporary Western culture – local culture in the third world is lost in this scenario. Of particular interest to questions of local agency, the homogenization scenario portrays the third world as defenceless and as taken by surprise by globalizing forces, unorganized and unprepared for the engagement with capitalism and metropolitan culture.[8] In the peripheral corruption scenario, the centre exports 'its high ideals and best knowledge' to the periphery which then corrupts and spoils them. This scenario, he argues, is very ethnocentric in the way it denies the validity and worth of transformations which occur at the periphery. Cultural difference is not recognized in the scenario; rather it is constructed as culture (centre) and non-culture (periphery), civilization and savagery.

Physical well-being is not the only relevant indicator or focus of analysis when considering security at the local level, or in a community setting. Factors such as identity, cultural practices and relationships with the natural environment may be significant in the consideration of individual and community group security. Understanding culture to be ubiquitous in social life and organized as a flow of meanings, through meaningful forms between people, Hannerz distinguishes four typical social frameworks in which cultural flows occur: the market, the state, forms of life and social movements (1991, pp. 112–16). Whilst we cannot explicate these in detail, a brief outline of his framework is fruitful, for his project attempts to engage with the 'totality of cultural process' through examining these individual flow movements and their interactions.

In the market framework, cultural commodities, primarily commodities with intellectual, aesthetic or emotional appeal, are transferred; 'meanings and meaningful forms are thus produced and disseminated by specialists in exchange for material compensation, setting up asymmetrical, more or less centring relationships between producers and consumers' (Hannerz, 1991, p. 112). The state framework of cultural process refers to its organizational form, the way in which it is engaged with the management of meaning;

the broad project to construct citizens culturally as members of a nation-state may involve both homogenization and production of difference, as is 'desirable for the purpose of fitting categories of individuals into different slots in the production and reproduction' (p. 113). The state framework is also asymmetrical with resources concentrated in, and flows of meaning emanating largely from, the centre.

Most importantly for micro-security is the framework of 'forms of life' which Hannerz understands to involve everyday practicalities of production and reproduction, activities in work areas, domestic spaces, neighbourhoods and so on. In this third framework, Hannerz's disciplinary home of anthropology influences the concentration in 'forms of life' on the 'distinctive' in local cultures and how 'experiences and interests coalesce into habitual perspectives and dispositions' through repetition of day-to-day goings-on – experiencing hearing and seeing the same things over and over in a locality. Significantly, Hannerz argues that some degree of 'cultural redundancy', or 'cultural autonomy' (pp. 114–15) can result from the strength of a form of life in a particular community, which is more difficult for cultural influence from the state or market to penetrate:

> The form of life framework has...a redundancy of its own, built up through its ever recurrent daily activities, perhaps at least as strong as, or stronger than, any redundancy that the market framework can ever achieve. There is perhaps a core here to which the market framework cannot reach, not even in the longer term, a core of culture which is not itself easily commoditized and to which the commodities of the market are not altogether relevant. (p. 123)[9]

This framework provides a critical method for those interested in looking at how the complex interrelations of the market, state and local communities impact on conditions of action under global conditions. One impact is how specific 'forms of life' are drawn into the world system in contradictory ways, both in temporal and in spatial terms, through the local division of labour and its relation to the international division of labour, and through cultural flows from centre to periphery. This can explain how some communities seem far more integrated with the world system in material, technological and cultural terms.[10]

In what ways then can we understand cultural identity, daily lived experiences and coping strategies as relevant or indeed significant for analysis of community security? Escobar sites one such example where a Latin American group of intellectuals and activists, the Andean Peasant

Technology Project (Proyecto Andino de Tecnologias Campesinas; PRATEC), have tried to explain 'some of the qualities of Andean culture and their validity for the majority of the people in the Peruvian Andes' which in turn they hope will 'contribute to the affirmation and autonomy of Andean culture' (Escobar, 1995, p. 169):

> Within the Andean worldview – in PRATEC's exposition – the peasant world is conceived of as a living being, with no separation between people and nature, between individual and community, between society and the gods. This live world continually recreates itself through mutual caring by all living beings. This caring depends on an intimate and ongoing dialogue between all living beings (including again, people, nature, and the gods), a sort of affirmation of the essence and will of those involved. This dialogue is maintained through continual interactions that are social and historical. (*ibid.*)

Although Andean knowledge and practices have been undermined by their encounter with modernity, PRATEC activists believe that many long-standing practices still exist and that peasants have kept their vision of the world whilst at the same time using some instruments of modernity (Escobar, 1995, p. 169). This is what Hannerz would see as the strategic redundancy of everyday practices in a particular cultural context. PRATEC's project, Escobar argues, ponders a process of affirmation and restructuring of Peruvian society based on anti-imperialism, re-peasantization, re-ethnicization, advancing strategies of decolonization and agrocentrism to strive for self-sufficiency in food (*ibid.*). This example brings together a number of important issues for micro-security – how cultural and historical factors affect the way in which people view their world and their position in it; how intervention based on generalizations and predetermined cures can exacerbate the problem; how people mediate external ideas with cultural practice to generate coping strategies and alternatives; how cultural affirmation and identity can be linked to their personal idea of security. These questions represent future avenues for research relating to identity, culture and security, not only relating to issues of the state, citizenship and nationalism, but also to the culture and identity literature in IR.

Lastly, moving away from politics as struggles of state-based territory to issues of complexity and difference in social systems, politics as resistance, or some form of empowerment, cannot be confused with speaking for the marginalized. Caution must be shown to the distinction between giving a voice to the marginalized in the security debate and the struggle of marginalized people. The political project of a micro-security approach in this way is to speak *in relation to* marginalized people. As Chow warns, we must

> find a resistance to the liberal illusion of the autonomy and independence we can 'give' the other... This means that *our* attempts 'to explore the other point of view' and 'to give it a chance to speak for itself,' as the passion of many current discourses goes, must always be distinguished from the other's struggles, no matter how enthusiastically we assume the non-existence of that distinction. (quoted in Escobar, 1995, p. 170)

Practical Contexts

How then might this framework be applied in an actual community context? Whether at the village level or other forms of community organization, coping and resistance strategies to a variety of circumstances, to cultural change, to economic vulnerability, through alignment with strategic partners like NGOs, form part of options open to communities to mitigate against insecurity. It also involves in many ways a participation process which may lead to greater autonomy. This autonomy could be in relation to government policy, to changing conditions of production, land loss, environmental factors (drought, floods), changing commodity prices, gender relations and so on. The ability to examine not only material factors which directly affect people's conditions of existence, but also the process through which survival and some forms of empowerment may take place, is central to a micro-security approach. It allows us to think about how conditions of existence may be related to security concerns and how they function within complex social systems.

Participatory Development Programmes: Connections Between Empowerment and Participation

Struggles against poverty – struggles to increase security – can be at once ecological struggles, gender struggles and struggles to maintain production conditions and identities. In this sense, there is a connection between poverty, nature, development, security, identity and strategies of resistance – resistance which may not be overtly political, but part of a complex relationship where contestations are also struggles for security. Formulating ways of understanding and explaining how the state is connected to these negotiations is an important task. Whilst there are arguments on both sides of the methodological fence for studying security (McSweeney, 1996; Buzan and Wæver, 1997), from an individualist/group approach or from the state/international system approach, there is ground to be gained from exploring ways in which they are, if not compatible, not entirely incommensurate.

The 'empowerment' of people in the third world, through grassroots organizations (GROs), participatory community development strategies of NGOs, state and international bodies, has been increasingly advocated as a 'means of enhancing the development process' (Mayo and Craig, 1995, p. 2). Here we might look at the way that community participation strategies that promote sustainable, people-centred development, equal opportunities and social justice could be linked to Booth's notion of emancipation as freeing people from the physical and human constraints which limit their security (Mayo and Craig, 1995, p. 1; Booth, 1991, p. 319). Mayo and Craig note the potential for both conflict and co-operation in the relations between community-based (grassroots) initiatives and development professionals (either state or NGO) and their interaction with the role of state and international bodies in the development process (1995, pp. 8–9). This raises important questions regarding the state's positive and/or negative role(s) in the development process and the politicization of security-orientated community initiatives for reform and change.

Participatory development strategies undertaken by NGOs in consultation with the community offer one practical context in which development concerns relate closely to community security issues. It is both the site of concrete measures to increase material living conditions in conjunction with community needs and the point at which the process of participation in development projects can facilitate greater community ownership of the project. The possibility that empowerment for poor people can emerge from these relationships is positive yet highly ambiguous. Empowerment is an ambiguous word in the development literature, one which has been critiqued on the assumption that power can be exchanged or transferred from NGO or development worker to the 'subjects of development' (Escobar, 1995, pp. 182–92). Nevertheless, participatory development programmes can provide access to resources and information, and poor people can increase their ability to participate in decision-making about their community's development. This is not to say that NGOs or development workers can ever know completely the position of the poor, or do not exert external influences in the process of indigenous/local development. However, it does suggest that community participation in autonomous development strategies, in conjunction with NGOs, can provide us with an alternative way of viewing change and security concerns as a process within that change.

Within this context, a micro-security approach is interested in looking at the complex interrelations between individuals, groups and mechanisms of the state which invariably affect the context of development at the community level. To suggest some examples, this can be through state policy on the internal actions of NGOs, state economic policy or extensions of the state in the form of mass organizations which work in and through the community. In various ways these connections are significant for security studies as a whole.

We agree that individual/community security approaches may not be able to fully grasp the securitization process at the international and state level – an argument put forward by Buzan and Wæver (1997) in their critique of a reductionist individualist security approach. However, should the discussion around securitization at these levels not acknowledge the domestic nature of inputs which affect formulation of state security policy? This book argues that security issues were and remain substantially different for the majority of third world states and people. It appears then that the nature of internal complexities around security are particularly pertinent for third world states, and for third world peoples which we have argued have been marginalized from the security debate in IR. Significantly, commentators within IR acknowledge critical and emancipatory security claims to be valid, but they lack the structural power to have their voices heard. More focus on the security issues at the community level may be able to examine the impact and importance of these less powerful voices through a more fluid conception of society than that of structural realism.

Conclusions

Theoretically, why is it important to retain a sense of agency for the poor and marginalized in security analysis? Whilst contradictions exist in trying to identify strategies and conditions under which people have decision-making capacity in their own lives, identification of those contradictions in the process is significant. Firstly, it is because we can acknowledge the contradictions as sites where this alternative agency scenario struggles with the dominant position occupied in this case by traditional security discourse. Secondly, it is because retaining a notion of agency allows us to take seriously the voices of the poor in agenda-setting and decision-making in their everyday lives as resistance and evidence of their own situated knowledges.

Developing a theoretical position around micro-security in a particular setting illustrates the importance of agency in the community, not only because it is part of an overall human process of development more generally, but also because to deny this agency leaves few alternatives to economistic or discursive/postmodern explanations of the development process. Without reverting to an individualistic-based security model, this chapter has tried to illustrate how the agency of the poor in the development process is politically significant in the process of allowing voices of the 'other' to be heard and also to fully recognize the 'real experience of development that is the conduct and change in daily livelihoods' (Saurin, 1996, p. 675). The recognition of this agency is significant in the process of uncovering micro-experiences of the development process, micro-experiences of community or group security, and in realizing the empowering role that recognition of community agency gives to more normative positions in security studies within IR.[11]

Notes

1. See David Booth's often-quoted article (1985), which argued that the 'new' Marxist-influenced development sociology of the early 1970s had reached an impasse, and that 'a key problem...is Marxism's metatheoretical commitment to demonstrating the "necessity" of economic and social patterns, as distinct from explaining them and exploring how they might be changed' (p. 761). See also Vandergeest and Buttel's neo-Marxist response (1988) which argued that the impasse in development sociology could be overcome by the application of a neo-Weberian tradition incorporating the work of Polanyi, Tilly, Giddens and Bourdieu, among others. They argued that these theorists 'overcome the problem of reifying "ideal types" and formal theorising by using theory in dialogue with empirical evidence' and that 'because it deals with power relations in the context of class, the state, cultural interpretation, and so on, can lead to realistic strategies for the empowerment of the less powerless' (Vandergeest and Buttel, 1988, p. 683). See also Long (1990), who argues that the 'supposed crisis' in contemporary development sociology – a multiplicity of paradigms and communities of scholars in social science – is based on important differences in epistemology which are unlikely to disappear. Following Kuhn, Long argues that while some historical periods are dominated by one theoretical paradigm, other periods 'manifest a wide range of possibilities and combinations' which are 'more conducive for exploring ways of "bridging" paradigms' (p. 19). It is to this juncture that the 'impasse' in

development theory refers. Rather than problematic, it can help 'develop new modes of conceptualising the complexities and dynamics of social life' within a framework, Long argues, that can incorporate in the same analysis an understanding of agency, power and structure (p. 19). See also Slater's (1990) response to this article. Other works which deal with the 'impasse' in development theory include Apter (1987) and Toye (1987).
2. See Dalby's chapter in Krause and Williams (1997, pp. 8–9) where he discusses the anomalies of national and military security approaches with individual well-being, including how feminist critiques have questioned who and what are being secured by national and international security policies.
3. For an in-depth analysis of these linkages see the classic arguments in Hoffman (1987). See also Krippendorf (1987) and Smith (1987).
4. See note 34 in Pasha (1996, pp. 640–2).
5. For a further recent critique of the global civil society thesis relating to collective identities and sovereignty, see Marden (1997).
6. See Chan (1997) where he argues that there remain three areas of ambiguity which have only tentative or limited space within the discipline of IR. These are the extent to which knowledge can be securely based epistemologically and consequently '[do] diverse ontologies result in multiple epistemologies?'; the extent that multiple epistemologies and multiple ontologies reflect a 'west versus the rest divide, so that the discipline, in its global appreciation, is only partial rather than universal'; and finally the extent to which the discipline can see itself in terms of a structure–agency problematic where the structure 'because of the revolt of agents is more multi-faceted before' (p. 108).
7. See also Booth (1995) where he considers human rights and the discipline of IR, as well as a more recent self-reflective piece (1997, pp. 83–119).
8. As Hannerz points out, this view completely ignores the continuous historical development of centre–periphery contacts, where the first world has been present in the consciousness of third world people for a longer time than third world people have been present in the minds of those in the first; 'the notion of the sudden engagement between the cultures of centre and periphery may thus be an imaginative by-product of the late awakening to global realities of many of us inhabitants at the centre' (1991, p. 110).
9. Hannerz also suggests that 'the strength of the culture existing in such reserves may be such that it also reaches back to penetrate into segments more directly and more extensively defined by the centre' (1991, p. 115).
10. Criticized for operating with an 'undifferentiated notion of culture' which 'confuses a variety of processes, practices and levels of analysis' (Wolff, 1991, p. 167), Hannerz's definition of the interrelations between frameworks is not clear; acknowledging himself that there is no one-to-one relationship between the specificity of cultural definition (forms of life supposedly) and degree of material integration with the world system (1991, p. 115).
11. This chapter was informed by fieldwork undertaken in Laos and Vietnam. More detailed case-study material will be included in Melissa Curley's forthcoming PhD dissertation. Many thanks to the staff at Community Aid Abroad in Australia and Laos for participating in this research.

References

Acharya, A. (1997) 'The periphery as the core: the third world and security studies'. In Krause, K. and Williams, M. (eds) *Critical Security Studies: Concepts and Cases*. London: UCL Press, pp. 299–327.

Allen, T. and Thomas, A. (eds) (1992) *Poverty and Development in the 1990s*. Oxford: Oxford University Press.

Apter, D. (1987) *Rethinking Development: Modernization, Dependency and Postmodern Politics*. London: Sage.

Ayoob, M. (1995) *The Third World Security Predicament*. Boulder, CO: Lynne Rienner.

Ayoob, M. (1997) 'Defining security: a subaltern realist perspective'. In Krause, K. and Williams, M. (eds) *Critical Security Studies: Concepts and Cases*. London: UCL Press, pp. 121–46.

Booth, D. (1985) 'Marxism and development sociology: interpreting the impasse', *World Development*, 13 (7), 761–87.

Booth, K. (1991) 'Security and emancipation', *Review of International Studies*, 17 (4), 313–26.

Booth, K. (1995) 'Human wrongs and international relations', *International Affairs*, 71 (1), 103–26.

Booth, K. (1997) 'Security and self: reflections of a fallen realist'. In Krause, K. and Williams, M. (eds) *Critical Security Studies: Concepts and Cases*. London: UCL Press, pp. 83–119.

Buzan, B. et al. (1990) *The European Security Agenda Recast: Scenarios for the Post-Cold War Era*. London: Pinter.

Buzan, B. and Wæver, O. (1997) 'Slippery? Contradictory? Sociologically untenable? The Copenhagen school replies', *Review of International Studies*, 23 (2), 241–50.

Buzan, B., Wæver, O. and De Wilde, J. (1997) *Security: New Frameworks for Analysis*. Boulder, CO: Lynne Rienner.

Chan, S. (1997) 'Seven types of ambiguity in western international relations theory and painful steps towards right ethics', *Theoria: A Journal of Social and Political Theory*, June, 106–15.

Dalby, S. (1997) 'Contesting an essential concept: reading the dilemmas in contemporary security discourse'. In Krause, K. and Williams, M. (eds) *Critical Security Studies: Concepts and Cases*. London: UCL Press, pp. 3–31.

Enloe, C. (1989) *Bananas, Beaches and Bases: Making Feminist Sense of International Politics*. London: Pandora.

Enloe, C. (1993) *The Morning After: Sexual Politics at the End of the Cold War*. Berkeley, CA: University of California Press.

Escobar, A. (1995) *The Making and Unmaking of the Third World*. Princeton: Princeton University Press.

Ferguson, J. (1990) *The Anti-Politics Machine: Development, Depoliticization and Bureaucratic Power in Lesotho*. Cambridge: Cambridge University Press.

Hannerz, U. (1991) 'Scenarios for peripheral cultures'. In King, A. (ed) *Culture, Globalization and the World System*. London: Macmillan, pp. 107–28.

Hoffman, M. (1987) 'Critical theory and the inter-paradigm debate', *Millennium: Journal of International Studies*, 16 (2), 231–49.

Kothari, R. (1993) *Poverty: Human Consciousness and the Amnesia of Development*. London: Zed Books.

Krippendorf, E. (1987) 'The dominance of American approaches in international relations', *Millennium: Journal of International Studies*, 16 (2), 207–29.

Long, N. (1990) 'From paradigm lost to paradigm regained? The case for an actor-oriented sociology of development', *European Review of Latin American and Caribbean Studies*, 49 (December), 3–24.

Marden, P. (1997) 'Geographies of dissent: globalization, identity and the nation', *Political Geography*, 16 (1), 37–64.

Mayo, C. and Craig, G. (1995) *Community Empowerment*. London: Zed Books.

McSweeney, B. (1996) 'Identity and security: Buzan and the Copenhagen school', *Review of International Studies*, 22 (1), 81–93.

Pasha, M. (1996) 'Globalization and poverty in South Asia', *Millennium: Journal of International Studies*, 25 (3), 635–56.

Pigg, S. (1992) 'Inventing social categories through place: social representations and development in Nepal', *Comparative Studies in Society and History*, 34 (3), 491–513.

Saurin, J. (1996) 'Globalization, poverty and the promises of modernity', *Millennium: Journal of International Studies*, 25 (3), 657–80.

Slater, D. (1990) 'Fading paradigms and new agendas: crisis and controversy in development studies', *European Review of Latin American and Caribbean Studies*, 49 (December).

Smith, S. (1987) 'Paradigm dominance in international relations: the development of IR as a social science', *Millennium: Journal of International Studies*, 16 (2), 189–206.

Sylvester, C. (1994) *Feminist Theory and International Relations*. Cambridge: Cambridge University Press.

Tickner, J. (1992) *Gender and International Relations: Feminist Perspectives on Achieving Global Security*. New York: Columbia University Press.

Tooze, R. and Murphy, C. (1996) 'The epistemology of poverty and the poverty of epistemology in IPE: mystery, blindness and invisibility', *Millennium: Journal of International Studies*, 25 (3), 681–707.

Toye, J. (1987) *Dilemmas of Development*. Oxford: Blackwell.

Vandergeest, P. and Buttel, F. (1988) 'Marx, Weber and developing sociology: beyond impasse', *World Development*, 16 (6), 683–95.

Wæver, O. et al. (eds) (1989) *European Polyphony: Perspectives beyond East–West Confrontation*. London: Macmillan.

Wæver, O. et al. (1993) *Identity, Migration and the New Security Agenda in Europe*. London: Pinter.

Walt, S. (1991) 'The renaissance of security studies', *International Studies Quarterly*, 35 (2), 211–37.

Wolff, J. (1991) 'The global and the specific: reconciling conflicting theories of culture'. In King, A. (ed.) *Culture, Globalisation and the World System*. London: Macmillan, pp. 161–73.

7

Security and Sustainable Development

In the previous chapter we have seen how the historical separation of International Relations (IR) and Development Studies (DS) has seen security and poverty effectively separated in theoretical discussion in the atomized social sciences. We have also seen how this separation might be overcome, especially in post-Cold War and poststructuralist IR, with potentially important and interesting consequences for any debate over security. In this context, and at first glance, *sustainable* development seems like an idea which will be able to resolve the artificial separation and to provide security in a multifaceted sense. As originally formulated, and as used most commonly by politicians, sustainable development claims to resolve environmental problems whilst at the same time addressing the necessity for economic growth. It thereby addresses 'new' security issues brought to the fore in the work of Buzan and Ayoob and significantly, in doing so, it also claims to be able to solve problems of inter- and intra-generational inequality, thus – following Burton (1972) – effectively removing the sources and possibility of conflict at various levels, and providing security in various military and non-military senses.

It is easy to see why sustainable development has been so popular with politicians. However, such an interpretation of the potential of the idea needs to come under some serious scrutiny. In order to evaluate this highly optimistic interpretation of the concept, this chapter stems from some of the others (especially 4 but also 3 and 5) and hopes to build on the previous one. In the first instance, if economics and the environment are amongst those factors to be included in wider conceptions of security, to what extent can a concept like sustainable development contribute to security, claiming as it often does to solve the contradictions between the two? Implicit in some work is the idea that uttering the words 'sustainable development' is somewhat like abracadabra; contradictions will be solved and we will all live happily ever after, economically and environmentally secure. However, such a position does not even entertain the question of what the words actually mean and whether there are competing conceptions. In this context we are particularly interested here as to whether there are any particular definitions or mediations of the idea that are likely to advance the people-centred security that we spoke of in the previous chapter. The present chapter hopes to deal with these issues. It is based partly on an analysis of the extent to which competing eco-philosophies (Chapter 4) are likely to influence the debate and partly on field research undertaken in Bolivia in 1997.

Sustainable development's implicit claim to provide security to humanity by resolving problems of inter- and intra-generational inequality effectively rests on its ability to lead us to an era of enhanced growth more equitably distributed but without sacrificing the world's environmental capital. In order to fully address the possibility for such a situation, this chapter looks at not only what sustainable development does mean in the politician's lexicon but also what it might mean. Accepting the previous chapter's analysis of the separation of IR (security) and DS (poverty) as well as the dangers of universalizing discourses, this chapter seeks to explore the extent to which sustainable development has the potential to close gaps and the extent to which, in some forms, it is able to escape the criticisms aimed at it by, amongst others, Escobar (1995).

This consideration of sustainable development in a security context is considered important because it is frequently being thrown together with phrases like human or true security as if the linkage were self-evident. It is not that such a potential linkage is denied here, more that sustainable development's roots in different types of *Northern* environmentalism (see Adams, 1990, 1995), plus the ways in which it is tied, or is *being tied*, to the development discourse need to be examined before we can specify in exactly which ways such development may be said to be in any sense similar to, or part of, people's security.

This chapter first seeks to look at the multiple usages of sustainable development. In its dominant conception it has been convincingly argued that

> the epistemological and political reconciliation of economy and ecology proposed by sustainable development is intended to create the impression that only minor adjustments to the market system are needed to launch an era of environmentally sound development, hiding the fact that the economic framework itself cannot hope to reform. Furthermore, by

rationalizing the defence of nature in economic terms, green economists continue to extend the shadow that economics casts on life and history. (Escobar, 1995, p. 197)

Sklair's observations that sustainable development is an attempt to shore up development against a critical tide are made in similar vein (Sklair, 1991). However, the history of the idea shows us that other currents, not tied to the development discourse, are contained within the idea; if minor adjustments to the capitalist world order in an era of globalization do not look promising in terms of improving people's security, then perhaps some of the alternative understandings of sustainable development offer more promise.

Having looked at the roots and usages of the term, we then move on to look at sustainable development in a concrete context. Any amount of eco-philosophizing is only relevant in the context of implementations or actualizations of the term.[1] Here we look at Bolivia, a country which initiated the world's first Ministry of Sustainable Development and Environment (Ministerio de Desarrollo Sostenible y Medio Ambiente; MDSMA); local definitions, adaptations and mediations are considered to see what promise the term holds for improving the real lives of real people. On the basis of this case-study material, combined with our analysis of differing conceptions and histories of sustainable development, we will be in a position to reflect upon the casual/causal linking of development and security and hopefully be able to specify with more precision the nature of any possible link.

What Is Sustainable Development?

It is easy to be quite sceptical about the concept of sustainable development and to see its political popularity in its *implication* of something radical (genuine change) without actually requiring it (Adams, 1990). Are we talking about a concept at all or a justification of neoliberalism that can be as flexible in its usage as democracy has been? Is this not simply another case of Western expert knowledge being imposed on the third world? After all, the development apparatus appears to have remained flexible over time, co-opting new historical and political situations under the development regime of truth and power (Escobar, 1995).

The first point to make is that although sustainable development has often been adopted by development practitioners of all kinds and also been pilloried in other quarters for its efforts to sustain 'development' as a term/idea(l) rather than representing a new concept, such development has arguably more roots in Northern environmentalism than developmentalism; and since Northern environmentalism is characterized by tensions between a dualism which is variously called environmentalism/ecologism, shallow ecology/deep ecology and reformism/radicalism (which for some may be more accurately characterized as a continuum)[2] these differences have subsequently been played out in discussions about what constitutes sustainable development. Since the reformist side of environmentalism has been strongest in the North, the voices of radicalism in the debate have been marginalized to the point of being, at times, almost silenced; nonetheless, they exist!

Furthermore, whilst the dominant core of Northern environmentalism has often been seen as a product of prosperity (the post-materialist thesis), we can also increasingly identify a Southern environmentalism, or environmentalism of the poor, growing out of distributional conflicts over ecological resources which are essential to people's lives. Such environmentalism is also seeking a voice within the sustainable development debate (Guha and Martinez-Alier, 1997). In short, the debate over what constitutes sustainable development is not simple and is, if anything, becoming more complicated.

In its reformist majority formulation (encapsulated best perhaps in the definition offered by the Brundtland Commission to which we return), Northern environmentalism lends to sustainable development a faith in technology to enable reform of current practices. Better planning and care can avoid ecological degradation, and growth can emerge through qualitative improvements rather than through increasing quantities. Science, rationality and management (the motivation for early conservation organizations was concerned with preserving 'white hunting' by preventing 'black poaching') combine to provide a cultural hegemony associated with environmental concerns and the concept of sustainable development (see Wilson and Bryant, 1997). In this sense, sustainable development is about preserving the status quo, about modifications to a neoliberal consensus, about making the market work, about growth to fund environmental protection and about getting the prices right. In a neoliberal utopia the end-point of this would be *relative* prosperity for all; however, in a survival of the fittest free market, where competition is absolutely essential to success, there would always be relative or absolute insecurity for the losers.

However, this is not the only way to understand sustainable development. Whilst Dobson (1995) is right to point out the grounds for regarding ecologism as a separate ideology and that attempts to argue that socialism has always been about the environment are stretching a point, it is nonetheless the case that in certain forms of social anarchism or utopian socialism we can find forerunners of a more radical 'deep green' ideology. The basis of such arguments has been summed up by Bookchin (1980), who argues that the current environmental crisis stems from the structure of the existing social framework.

> In other words, there are currents which, when applied to sustainable development, will want to argue that new forms of social organization will be necessary if we are to resolve ecological contradictions, thus rejecting Brundtland's implicit message that 'economic growth, renamed "sustainable development", is a remedy for both poverty and environmental degradation'. (Guha and Alier-Martinez, 1997, p. 46)

In looking at the third world, arguments are frequently emerging that the dominant Northern conception of sustainable development is, in fact, a trick to maintain a system of injustice. However, in some respects Southern environmentalism mirrors that in the North by having a dominant conception that sees the need for continued, indefinite and more forceful growth and a subordinate current associated particularly with local struggles and grassroots organizations (GROs) that is the environmentalism of the poor referred to previously.

In light of the above, and looking at sustainable development in practice, there are two pronounced types of vision or actualizations which we can identify. One is consumer/growth orientated – encapsulated in the eco-audit/eco-labelling approach of the European Union (EU). We are encouraged to demand cleaner, greener, dishwashers and cars, but always more of them. Efficiency is the key, and business has been dragged along, not unwillingly, at a comfortable pace that allows continuing profits in the short term whilst ensuring competitiveness in the longer. Industrial society is left unchanged; whole countries are convinced that they are doing their bit, but are societies facing the truth?[3] Cars today are hugely more efficient than the first ones of a hundred years ago, but their net impact on the environment is also much greater; the tendency of technological efficiency to overcome limits to consumption rather than helping us live within ecological limits is little acknowledged by neoliberal triumphalism. Technicist myths make the emperor a very fine suit indeed, and there are plenty in the South looking to use the same tailor.

Since the dominance of liberal values seems so entrenched that some claim there is no going back and no alternative, the space for manoeuvre of those who would suggest a different social order are very much limited. Accordingly, the more radical versions of sustainable development are, in any larger sense, little more than academic visions. However, at local levels, especially in communities living at the cutting edge of the ecological crisis, projects which do encapsulate a radical alternative are emerging as local responses or sites of resistance to a bulldozing neoliberal orthodoxy. Such approaches do not necessarily reject the Enlightenment rationality which has led us to environmental crisis because it is not rational but because it is not enlightened. Thus, throughout Latin America, communities campaign against mining which poisons rivers or against inadequate urban water supplies.

A major point to be made here is that for both technocratic and radical versions of sustainable development there is a clear break between theory and practice. Reformist sustainable development claims to be something new and offers a solution to the crisis; however, in practice it defends traditional notions of development (growth as the means to the wealth to protect the environment) and offers not solutions but short-term ameliorations (*at best*) to the worst effects of the crisis. In theory the radical formulation suggests radical reorganizations of global society and production as the solution; unfortunately, in practice it is unable to do more than operate in those small spaces which it is able to lever open in the neoliberal dominance of political discourse. This is a point which will be returned to in the concluding chapter.

The environmental movement then, such as it exists, is a complex and confusing mix of modernism and anti-modernism as well as acceptance, rejection or modification of the Enlightenment project, and sustainable development is an inheritor of this confusion (Adams, 1995, p. 98). Perhaps one useful way to look at this confusion is to suggest that while '*sustained* development is an economic concept based on an expectancy of economic growth the ecological concept of *sustainable* development is concerned with viable continuity into the long term'. The former (*sustained* development) tends towards the 'dictum of maximum sales [and] means the briefest possible use and the cheapest possible construction. It means advertising to create a need for consumption. It means replacement not repair, planned obsolescence not reuse. It means emphasis on export and long haulage of goods across the globe' (Adam, 1994, p. 107). To the extent that it is this conception which is dominating understandings of sustainable development, and in looking at the evolution of the environment as an issue area around which is forming a new social movement as part of a global civil society, the contradictions are reflected in the following conundrum: whether to regard a global civil society as a reinforcing mechanism (as did Gramsci in a national context) for the global capitalist order or as a site of potential and collective resistence against the worst excesses of it (Germain and Kenny, 1998). At the very least, 'the difficulties of generalising from the social movements of the "developed" countries to the Third World... The great differences in the complex problems faced in those countries clearly indicates a different pattern of emergence of environmental social movements, and the necessity for more research' (Redclift and Benton, 1994, p. 22).

Many of the points raised above are returned to in the concluding chapter. For now it is enough to outline the nature of the debate about what sustainable development might be as a prelude to the next section which looks at the way sustainable development has been embraced in the particular context of Bolivia. This section is considered particularly important. It is one thing to say that security would be achieved if liberal dreams of what sustainable development means were realizable, at least for the majority, rather than, as now, the minority. It is similarly possible to say that community empowerment or 'deep green bio-regional communalism' could provide security in a different sense of ecological balance and spiritual fulfilment. However, the connections between sustainable development and security, such as they exist, can only really be evaluated in terms of how the former is being implemented, and how it might be changing things, in concrete contexts. As a country which takes regional, if not global pride in its wholehearted embrace of sustainable development, Bolivia is considered an appropriate place to begin consideration of this matter.

Sustainable Development in Bolivia

Influential socialist turned green, Rudolf Bahro was forced to leave the German Democratic Republic for suggesting that it should stop growth competition with the West. He subsequently left the West German greens for their obsession with electoral politics rather than principle. He is reluctant to travel by air.[4] He suggests that the success of the human species, if it can be regarded as such, resembles the success of a plague of locusts and calls for spiritual regeneration and an accompanying eco-philosophy (Bahro, 1994). His views are popular in some university classrooms but, for others, represent exactly the kind of 'utopian eco-reflection' which seems out of place when faced with the realities and necessities of many countries throughout the third world (see Vogler, 1996). Here then we look at sustainable development in practice rather than as the eco-utopia that we might like it to become, either in a reformist/liberal or in a radical/deep green sense. In doing so, we do not argue that vision is not crucial in leading us from environmental crisis nor do we condone the reformism of Brundtland. Rather, this is simply a recognition that, in whichever guise, sustainable development is increasingly dominating policy-making discourse throughout many countries of the world and its effects must therefore be considered in thinking about security.

Accordingly, whilst accepting comments about the dangers of sustainable development becoming another universalizing discourse of more harm than good in its application to the third world, this section also wants to pick up the claim, in a sustainable development context, that understanding dependence is much more about understanding the room to manoeuvre within it as it is about understanding the chain of dependence – that internal factors must remain a focus whatever the wider structures (Randall and Theobald, 1985). Recent academic rejections of the whole development discourse, including sustainable development, have been numerous. However, even if we were to accept such a proposition as unproblematic, and that interventions based on generalizations and predetermined cures can often exacerbate problems, it is also surely the case that people mediate external ideas with cultural practice to generate coping strategies and alternatives.

Hence, in focusing on Bolivia we have sought to examine how the sustainable development idea has been manifest, how it is perceived by different sectors and groups and how this idea (or concept or extension of the development discourse) is mediated through specific local situations. Broadly speaking, the hope is to outline the complex interactions between various sectors of Bolivian society and to specify which processes are associated with the concept of sustainable development in the country. We look at the extent to which the United Nations Conference on Environment and Development (UNCED) model has been applied in Bolivia and the extent to which it has been successful. Opinions vary between enthusiastic endorsement (Jarmuz Levy *et al.*, 1996), albeit within the context of limited resources, to condemnation of an idea brought from abroad but poorly understood and implemented without genuine commitment.[5] Within this context, it is important to look at what is distinctive about this concept in a local context: what constitutes *Bolivian* sustainable development, how is it understood by Bolivians and what advances and regressions it represents compared with previous notions of development and the political systems with which they were associated.[6]

In terms of the embrace and implementation of the UNCED model, Bolivia is clearly ahead of the game in a regional, if not global context. Lacking a strong, prosperous economy, if not resources, there is perhaps as good a rationale here, as anywhere, to try something new. What is more debatable is the extent to which the idea has permeated the consciousness of more than a tiny minority, even of educated and prosperous elite groups. For most Bolivians, *desarrollo* and *sostenible* are simply words, and words with which they are not familiar at that. When the struggle for existence is paramount, survival becomes the key, such that planning for sustainable development in three months or a year, let alone for future generations, becomes impossible.[7] Short-term security must take priority over any longer-term meaning.

However, Bolivia *appears* to have a solid legal and governmental structure as the basis for an environmentally sound development, or rather one that casts a lighter ecological shadow. Amongst approved and significant laws in the 1990s are the environmental law (no. 1333, 1992), the law of popular participation (no. 1551, 1994), a forestry law (no. 1700, 1996), an agrarian reform (no. 1715, 1996), and a recently approved mining code.[8] In 1993 the MDSMA was set up by the current government and in 1996 the government also formed the Bolivian Sustainable Development Council (Consejo Boliviano de Desarrollo Sostenible; CBDS) which is made up of representatives from a wide range of Bolivian society, including government, the military, peasant organizations, non-governmental organizations (NGOs), academics, students and so on.[9]

Despite such a promising start on paper, Bolivia is quite clearly not in the process of performing a miracle. Many of the new laws actually conflict with each other in various ways, or lack co-ordination, despite the role that the MDSMA is supposed to play in this regard. It is hardly surprising that matters have not worked smoothly when changes of administration bring radical restructuring of departments and wholesale changes of personnel, where appointments are based on political allegiance rather than technical know-how. Political patronage and the political system do not help; the nascent civil service is very weak, there is a widespread expectation that political loyalty *should* bring rewards and even the cleaners change with administration.

The original salience of sustainable development seems to have come from the then president's daughter and a very small group around a president who was largely brought up in the United States. Significantly then, the concept of sustainable development is linked very closely with the 1993–97 government, so that the previous president (now a junior partner in the present administration), whose government worked hard to introduce the environment law, now works equally hard to use any combination of words so long as they are *not* sustainable and development (in that order) (Movimeinto Boliviano Izquierdista, 1997). In fact, sustainable development appears to have been used as a buzzword in the aftermath of Rio but quickly lost its vote-pulling power and, whilst attracting sources of foreign investment, has led to very high levels of per capita debt.

After an initial burst of enthusiasm the government of Sanchez de Lozada seemed to lose interest in its own creation; the MDSMA was handed to a coalition partner and has not been adequately funded since. The government's policy *could*, in fact, be characterized as one of ensuring a good image abroad to ensure that new funds arrive, in the context of indebtedness.[10] The government appeared to set much stall by showpiece international events such as the summit at Santa Cruz in 1996, its attendance at the recent Rio +5 talks (with a joint government–civil society delegation) as well as the setting up of the CBDS. The CBDS, emphasized by the government as one of its big initiatives and achievements (established 1996), is referred to by others as something which the government initially resisted but eventually acceded to because of demands from civil society. These are strongly contrasting views, but the CBDS does appear to help project the *image* of a full consultative process enthusiastically embraced. However, in terms of a process of consultation it appears that this was much wider under the previous government in drafting the 1992 environmental law than it has been since.

To sum up the negative side of sustainable development in Bolivia outside government, it is perhaps the most commonly heard opinion on the subject within the country that 'the only thing sustainable in Bolivia is poverty' (see, for example, Central Obrera Boliviana, *c.* 1995).[11] This is not altogether a surprise and neither would be the conclusion that sustainable development operates in Bolivia very much as Escobar (1995) suggests in order to legitimate the importance of economics and to defend the entrenched interests of neoliberalism and the development apparatus. Certainly, despite much intellectual justification for the term, it is often still based on a messianic, and surely misplaced, belief in the market to produce, single-handedly, the miracle of sustainable development.[12]

Nevertheless, it seems necessary to go beyond such observations or conclusions in the case of Bolivia; that whatever the legitimizing usages of the term 'sustainable development' and however much reality fails to live up to the legal framework on paper, there are positive aspects to the whole process. This is not only because in the context of sustainable development Bolivia certainly does seem to be taking a lead in Latin America, if not globally (the MDSMA being the first of its kind in the world). However imperfect the process, each department (regional administrative unit) has drawn up, after a reasonably broad consultative process, an Agenda 21 action plan and it was the only country at recent Rio +5 meetings with a report written by government and civil society working together.[13] Furthermore, there are aspects of Bolivia's attitude to sustainable development which seem to have widespread support and an importance which goes beyond relevance to a limited local elite.

In terms of the distinctive application of this concept, idea or discourse, perhaps the most interesting ideas are encompassed in the notion of governability. This represents, according to its advocates, the fourth pillar of sustainable development in Bolivia, with the other three pillars being the tripod which represents the core of the Brundtland definition of the term,[14] namely economic growth, social equity (intra- and inter-generational) and environmental protection (rational use of natural resources). The analogy of a table was used to suggest that these four pillars must be co-ordinated in order to keep the top stable.[15] Within governability we are talking about a strong element of decentralization and the notion of popular participation whereby real resources (financial) are finally being channelled to all areas of Bolivia (311 municipalities in total). Popular participation stems, it is claimed, from the very reasonable assumption that poverty is a big cause of environmental degradation. For green political theorists such as Eckersley, who talks of the need for multi-layered government in the protection of the environment, or the more general green claim that small-scale democratic communities are the most likely to produce sustainable practices within the limits set by a finite planet, all this is clearly positive (see Hayward, 1994).

However, this idea is not universally lauded ('popular participation means everyone can take a chain saw to the forest'[16]) and, whilst it can be attacked as legitimation rather than substance, it does seem to be the aspect of the whole process taken most seriously by all sectors and the one aspect which does not seem purely and simply reliance on the market miracle. Certainly, one important peasant grouping spoken to criticized popular participation at the outset but became happier that it involved a genuine participatory power-sharing exercise.

Popular participation has not always been a total success. Many newly moneyed municipalities did not start to plan rational, environmentally sound use of their resources but began instead by building football pitches or repaired and brightened up the town square, not unreasonably given previous distribution of resources. However, popular participation and sustainable development have been accompanied by a process of education and an educative reform which has actually looked at curricula content rather than the number of schools. With the plaza looking tidy there is some statistical evidence to suggest that productive projects are now being introduced and that people now feel they have some stake in their own future (Rojas Ortuste and Verdesoto Custode, 1997).[17] Departmental governments and local communities are working together to see what can be achieved within this context of admittedly limited resources. Popular participation, whilst far from perfect, appears both irreversible and beneficial to Bolivian society.

In concluding this section, we do not disagree with the contention that the

> real losers in the battles on this discursive field [a]re all of those groups unable to muster sufficient technical expertise to make themselves heard, that is, lower classes and popular movements that [do] not have the resources to compete in a debate in which issues [are]...defined as technical matters to be resolved by experts. (Conaghan, 1996, p. 44)

However, there does seem to be a widespread recognition within Bolivia that sustainable development is a case of Bolivia doing what it is able within the constraints of neoliberalism; that as much as the concept is the latest Western/Northern trick to sell the development discourse, it is also Bolivia's latest trick to attract investment from abroad – for some people attracting foreign investments and creaming off the profits is more or less a profession.[18] Whilst with time it appears that the environmental component of the concept gets downgraded, partly as a result of the lack of a separate environmental ministry and also because of the necessities of the Bolivian situation (environmental disasters such as Taiwan are cited as models but not for environmental reasons), in broader terms the introduction of the idea of sustainable development has involved a healthy dose of self-criticism in Bolivia's young democracy which has seen this democracy extended and made genuinely more participatory. Although the case should not be overstated, especially given recent changes in government, Bolivia's history of 'thefts' of its national territory makes the notion of decentralization somewhat threatening to governmental elites, and the fact that it is happening at all is therefore highly significant (Lewis and Wigen, 1997).

Conclusions

The conclusions offered above will certainly be more optimistic than many Bolivians are currently able to be. On the other hand, the explicit and implicit criticisms offered will upset the true believers in the process. The main point to materialize as far as we are concerned is that we can neither discount a link between sustainable development and human security nor claim it to be self-evident. Sustainable development is *not* a miracle cure but in the Bolivian context has involved *some* redistribution of money and power. Nor must we become bogged down over whether 'sustainable development' as an ideal type would provide 'ideal' security. However, there is certainly evidence to suggest that sustainable development may lead to positive effects and help to empower local people who are asked to set their own priorities. On the other hand, the term is undoubtedly used to justify existing practices, especially by business, and helps to fend off any genuine challenges to the current developmentalist and growth-based model.

We live in an age in which Fukuyaman certainty is overwhelming. The West has retaken the moral high ground, chastising the South for the lack of efficacy of its 'alternative developments' and suggesting that, but for some environmental tinkering, it has a monopoly on truth, this time beyond dispute or quibble (Lewis, 1998). Certainly, to the extent that sustainable development provides the justification for a reformist approach and to the extent that it is simply a renaming of economic growth, we might consider it inadequate in addressing issues of environmental and human security, sustaining as it does a growth model which leads to degradation of the environment and injustice/inequality. On the other hand, currents within Northern environmentalism, which have now fed through to sustainable development, offer more hope. Ecologism offers not only the hope of a stable ecology but also the reorganization of human societies; security here becomes concerned not with some satisfaction of basic human needs but with genuine empowerment and emancipation of individuals.

As Hayward (1994) suggests in his arguments, the environmentalist injunction to 'think globally and act locally' may sound somewhat glib. However, there is a real sense in which large-scale problems must be broken down at source if they are to be effectively addressed. Furthermore, some of Bahro's optimism concerning the setting up of communes to act as examples and 'liberated zones' may seem far-fetched, but it is certainly the case that a spiritual awakening is more likely to *emerge* rather than spontaneously enveloping humanity, and that local examples of ecological resistence are developing in spaces created within traditional notions of development and the conventional notion of sustainable development. As Hayward points out, 'decentralization is so important [because] it means hierarchies are broken down and people are empowered' (1994, p. 188). Furthermore, adopting an ecological position means adopting the feminist notion of politicizing the personal:

> lifestyle changes can be seen as part of a broader strategy to transform and enrich the very concept of the political, and thereby to increase the sense, and reality, of empowerment of those hitherto excluded from politics in its mainstream definition. (Hayward, 1994, p. 196)

Finally therefore, in talking about the interrelated ideas of need (spiritual as well as material), ecological balance and what security might involve, whilst we may take some hope from the participatory and other positive aspects of sustainable development, it is nonetheless the case that this overused phrase currently signifies very little in terms of new security agendas in the third world, although it may be thrown together with human security as if some genuine link is implied. On the other hand, sustainable development from an ecological perspective offers greater hope of linking the idea to human security. Unfortunately, only by further playing out of the environmental contradictions inherent in current practices (something which is likely to have severe individual consequences, especially in the third world)[19] are we likely to see a less market-orientated sustainable development emerge. What is offered here is an invitation to think about sustainable development in theory and practice and about whether or not there is any value in linking the term to security or if this is simply a further complication in thinking what security might mean.

Notes

1. Here we effectively reject Habermas and argue that such practical knowledge is needed as the basis for a more critical knowledge.
2. Tim Hayward argues that these ideas are different but could profit from a constructive engagement (see Hayward, 1994).
3. For evidence of complacency over environmental matters in the Netherlands (an embedded shallow environmentalism), see Pettiford *et al.* (1997).

4. Air travel alone is responsible for 3 per cent of global CO^2 emissions.
5. For example, a range of opinions offered by Gonzalo Zambrana and his colleagues at the Centre for Ecology, Environment and Development of San Simon University, Cochabamba (series of interviews, 17–19 March 1997). Lloyd Pettiford gives his special thanks to all at the centre.
6. Information contained within this section uses information and opinions encountered during interviews by Lloyd Pettiford in Bolivia. Since in most cases these interviews were conducted on the basis that frank opinions would not be attributed, indication is sometimes given in subsequent footnotes simply that the views were offered rather than being those of the author.
7. Just one of a range of useful comments made by M. del Castillo, Head of Environment and Development, Municipal Government of Cochabamba (personal interview, 17 March 1997).
8. F. Loyaza Careaga, Subsecretary for Mines, Ministry for Economic Development, La Paz (personal interview, 11 April 1997).
9. Although the meeting attended was almost entirely dominated by government, elite NGOs and the ringing of mobile telephones.
10. This opinion was offered, without necessarily implying agreement, by E. Forno at the Conservation Data Centre, La Paz (personal interview, 6 March 1997).
11. Reiterated in interview with the Central Obrera Boliviana, Cochabamba, 17 March 1997.
12. Anonymous interview.
13. However, at both national and local levels, various peasant groupings, understandably cautious about motives and requesting anonymity, expressed various levels of dissatisfaction with the allegedly consultative process, generally suggesting that being asked what you thought did not lead to a genuine situation of compromise or consensus.
14. This was expressed by, amongst others, Dr Alejandro Mercado, National Co-ordinator of Bolivia's Capacity 21 Programme, La Paz (personal interview, 5 March 1997).
15. J. Rivera, Subsecretary for Development Strategy, MDMSA, La Paz (personal interview, 7 March 1997).
16. Anonymous interview with foreign aid worker.
17. Also personal interview with G. Rojas Ortuste, 13 April 1997.
18. Various anonymously expressed views.
19. Just as rich states such as the Netherlands are more able to protect themselves against sea-level rises than poorer ones such as the Maldives, rich individuals have the means to isolate or protect themselves from the worst excesses of the environmental crisis, often contributing further to the problem in the process through, for example, foreign air travel.

References

Adam, B. (1994) 'Running out of time: global crisis and human engagement'. In Redclift, M. and Benton, T. (eds) *Political Change and Underdevelopment: A Critical Introduction to Third World Politics*. London: Macmillan, Chapter 5.

Adams, W. M. (1990) *Green Development*. London: Routledge.

Adams, W. M. (1995) 'Green development theory: environmentalism and sustainable development'. In Crush, J. (ed.) *Power of Development*. London: Routledge, pp. 87–99.

Bahro, R. (1994) *Avoiding Social and Ecological Disaster: The Politics of World Transformation: An Enquiry into the Foundations of Spiritual and Ecological Politics*. Bath: Gateway Books.

Bookchin, M. (1980) *Toward an Ecological Society*. Montreal: Black Rose Books.

Burton, J. (1972) *World Society*. Cambridge: Cambridge University Press.

Central Obrera Boliviana et al. (undated, c. 1995) *Construyendo el Futuro: 25 Opiniónes Sobre Desarrollo Sostenible en Bolivia*. La Paz: Ministerio de Desarrollo Sostenible y Medio Ambiente.

Conaghan, C.M. (1996) 'A deficit of democratic authenticity: political linkage and the public in Andean politics', *Studies in Comparative International Development*, 31 (3), 32–55.

Dobson, A. (1995) *Green Political Theory*, 2nd edition. London: Routledge.

Escobar, A. (1995) *Encountering Development: The Making and Unmaking of the Third World*. Princeton: Princeton University Press.

Germain, R. and Kenny, M. (1998) 'Engaging Gramsci: international relations theory and the new Gramscians', *Review of International Studies*, 24 (1), 3–22.

Government of Bolivia (1992) *Ley del Medio Ambiente*. La Paz: Government of Bolivia.

Government of Bolivia (1995) *Ley de Participación Popular*. La Paz: Cultura Cívica.

Government of Bolivia (1996) *Ley Forestal*. La Paz: Government of Bolivia.

Government of Bolivia (1996) *La Ley INRA*. La Paz: Government of Bolivia.

Guha, R. and Martinez-Alier, J. (1997) *Varieties of Environmentalism: Essays North and South*. London: Earthscan.

Hayward, T. (1994) *Ecological Thought: An Introduction*. Oxford: Polity Press.

Jarmuz Levy, M. et al. (1996) *Building Sustainable Development*. La Paz: Ministerio de Desarrolle Sostenible y Medio Ambiente.

Lewis, M.W. and Wigen, K.E. (1997) *The Myth of Continents: A Critique of Metageography*. Berkeley: University of California Press.

Lewis, N. 'Globalisation and sovereignty: implications for the third world state'. In Poku, N. and Pettiford, L. (eds) (1998) *Redefining the Third World*. Basingstoke: Macmillan, pp. 88–106.

Movimiento Boliviano Izquierdista (1997) *Una Alianza Estratégica con los Bolivianos*. La Paz: Movimiento Boliviano Izquierdista.

Pettiford, L. et al. (1997) *Euro-Trash: The Televisual Representation of Environmental Issues in Three European Countries*. Nottingham: CRICC.

Randall, V. and Theobald, R. (1985) *Political Change and Underdevelopment: A Critical Introduction to Third World Politics*. London: Macmillan.

Redclift, M. and Benton, T. (eds) (1994) *Social Theory and the Global Environment*. London: Routledge.

Rojas Ortuste, G. and Verdesoto Custode, L. (1997) *La Participación Popular como Reforma de la Política: Evidencias de una Cultura Democrática Boliviana*. La Paz: Ministerio de Desarrollo Humano.

Sklair, L. (1991) *Sociology of the Global System*. London: Harvester Wheatsheaf.

Vogler, J. (1996) 'The politics of the global environment'. In Bretherton, C. and Ponton, G. (eds) *Global Politics: An Introduction*. Oxford: Blackwell, pp. 194–220.

Wilson, G.A. and Bryant, R.A. (1997) *Environmental Management: New Directions for the Twenty-first Century*. London: UCL Press.

Conclusions: The Future of Security?

In many countries throughout the world, still thought of and denominated as the 'third world' in popular media, the list of problems faced by people and the state is enormous. By tacking the word 'security' on to each of these problems some analysts have expanded the idea of third world security. Thus we have the appearance of terms such as food security, water security, health security, environmental security and so on; population becomes a security issue, as well as migration, urbanization, pesticide use and so on. Such an approach may well have value in terms of highlighting serious problems; we do not deny their existence, their importance and their links to what security might be and how it can be attained.

Others have assumed that such problems would be solved with state-building and have concentrated on the problems associated with this in the context of third world (that is poorer) states. Again, the value of much of this work is not questioned. What we have attempted here, however, is a synthesis of arguments surrounding security as a basis for thinking critically and constructively about a concept and associated debate which have tended towards the shapeless. We have tied our analysis to a preference for prioritizing a particular way of thinking when answering the question: how do we understand security?

This book has made much of the need to re*think* security rather than to re-*define* it. Whilst this distinction may seem like an unnecessary exercise in semantics, we believe that the job of re-definition is one which is effectively being carried out, at all levels of international relations, in the form of changing agendas for peoples, communities, states, regions and so on. Since agendas will change and vary, a single new definition is then, in any case, impossible. What is possible is a choice regarding which agenda or agendas to prioritize. What we suggest is a normative commitment to the third world, the poor and the marginalized, combined with a scholarly commitment to think through the issue of security in a manner more critical than simply seeing insecurity in terms of basic needs, for instance. This exercise in active and critical reflection is, we believe, necessary because, as we have noted earlier, 'no other concept in international relations packs the metaphysical punch, nor commands the disciplinary power of "security"'. Leading on from this, and somewhat ironically, changes in international relations must now question exactly how secure this pre-eminent concept of International Relations (IR) is (Der Derian, 1993, pp. 94–5).

Accordingly, in simple terms this book has hopefully achieved a number of things. First, it has demonstrated ways in which a simply understood and explained realist concept of security has been subject to sustained critique, leading to a variety of understandings of this once central organizing concept of the discipline of IR; within this we have argued that simple redefinitions (renamings) such as environmental security or global security need to be treated with caution. When examined carefully it becomes apparent that they are often underpinned by a multiplicity of different philosophies and ideas. In this way, seemingly radical/subversive ideas such as 'food security' can be interpreted in a manner which makes them supportive of the status quo.

Whilst aware of this danger, we have, secondly, tried to show how newer understandings of security, of various kinds, can be seen to have had greater relevance to what has been termed the 'third world' because of their normative commitments and subversiveness in relation to dominant discourses. In doing so, we have suggested that this term, the 'third world', is itself shifting because of various factors: the obvious differentiation between its broad range of countries; the globalization of production; the non-existence of a 'second world' in the post-Cold War world; and so on.

The logic for considering these two shifting patterns of terms together, which once had 'certain', 'fixed', or at least widely understood meanings, may now be apparent. Whilst the security debate has increasingly moved from the state-centric problem-solving of the traditional definition, to approaches which seek to stress the emancipatory potential of the idea in terms of marginalized groups, the third world has also shifted; no longer is it *seen* as a homogenous group of states (which of course it never was) but can be used as a means to identify (with), in much more than a state-centric way, those states, nations, communities and individuals in some sense marginalized or disempowered in the face of today's global political and economic forces. Hence these are the reasons for the linkages between security and poverty (discussed in Chapter 6) and security and the resistance/ influence of ecological movements (discussed in Chapters 4 and 7).

Before suggesting some implications, it is worth outlining briefly the main arguments of the book. The Introduction had the difficult task of suggesting the problematic without giving the game away. First, it outlined a traditional orthodoxy in the historical treatment of security by IR, and then sought to sketch certain aspects of the debate which has ensued, flagging the major themes and questions addressed by the book.

In suggesting the need to rethink the third world as those who are marginalized, and not just states, Chapter 1 provided us with a fluid, but ultimately more useful, concept to work with. 'Third world' now has meaning in local, national, regional and global contexts. It is composed of individuals, communities, states, nations and continents. Crucially, it becomes a relative rather than an absolute concept – one in which statistical indicators only indicate rather than being sole arbiters and in which geographical ring-fencing becomes inappropriate.

Chapter 2 on neorealism basically outlined a holding operation by orthodox IR. We argued that though various authors have done work that assigns the third world a more prominent role, this is still a state-based third world in which the interests of ordinary people are subordinated, and in which the truths of development in a global economy are left unquestioned. We suggested that the appearance of radicalism offered by various neorealist authors did, in a way which echoes various aspects of political history, manage to stave off genuinely radical critique.

However, neorealism's holding operation could only be temporary. Chapter 3 deals with IR's 'third debate' and those approaches which have gone beyond neorealism to ask such genuinely critical questions – namely, critical, postmodern and feminist approaches, frequently subsumed by the label poststructuralism. Critical perspectives ask what possible alternatives exist, whilst postmodernism is drawing our attention to difference and the impossibility of unicausality and meta-theory in our analysis of the third world. Within the broad category of feminism, many of the most influential analyses have come from such poststructuralist work.

Chapters 4 and 5 attempted to argue that IR could enrich its security debate by being genuinely inter-disciplinary. Chapter 4 looked at what might be regarded as a new issue in IR. We argued that looking at the philosophical underpinnings of the 'environment' has potentially much which may be of value to IR's security debate. Conversely, adopting conventional state-based attitudes may fail to advance our thinking or the cause of the global environment. In Chapter 5 we looked mainly at Peace Studies (PS) and argued that much work that has been done on the idea of peace could have fed earlier into thinking on security. The aim of considering the environment and PS (and to a lesser extent Political Geography) was partly to suggest some ways into the security debate, but primarily to argue that IR can no longer 'hide' from the rest of social science reassured by (un)comfortable certainty. Sociology and Cultural Studies, for instance, are also particularly likely to offer insight.

Finally, Chapters 6 and 7 have represented some work in progress. Rather than suggesting it as anything more, we have tried here to show how the use of non-positivist epistemology or the consideration of environmental issues, for example, can lead to very different work, nonetheless within the broad category of security studies. Our aim, as we have restated throughout, has not been a redefinition of security, and Chapters 6 and 7 do not claim to do this; they are more a practical demonstration of thinking about an idea. Beyond this, we hope that this book will stimulate further thinking and debate; some conjecture regarding relevant points for enquiry are suggested below.

Future Directions: Some Conjecture on the State of the Debate

Implicit in our approach is the idea that depending on the tools used there may be many different ways in which security may develop in the future. For instance, it could do so by continuing to work within traditional parameters, by incorporating insights and blending traditions and so on. Questions are raised for us, not only of what security is but also of how certain issues and actors become securitized by policy-making or academic communities and others do not. Explicit in our approach is a call for a more critical security and a security studies community prepared to engage seriously with the individual as unit of analysis and the way in which the individual and community levels interact with more traditional state-level approaches. Developing from some of the major arguments of the book, this position has a number of implications for the security debate, theoretically, regarding research methods in IR and in relation to the politics of studying security in IR as a discipline, and in relation to the third world.

First, the book has emphasized how and why it is important, indeed crucial, to consider how the individual and community level is significant in third world security issues. It raises the question of the epistemological implications of placing 'community' at the centre of an approach to security within the third world. This is not to say that it could not be compatible with other approaches which operate at the state and/or international level of analysis. However, it does highlight the need within the security debate to consider what linkages may be involved with understanding what has been seen largely as incongruous positions of analysis (see McSweeney, 1996; Buzan and Wæver, 1997). For IR it does mean at least understanding politics as about more than *territorial* community, and this requires the security debate to open itself to a discussion about how community is defined by issues of culture and identity.

The discussion within the discipline around culture and identity is becoming broader (Lapid and Kratochwil, 1997; Krause and Renwick, 1996) and it is not possible in this conclusion to outline in any detail how it relates to community and individual security. Despite the increasing engagement with issues of culture and identity, it appears that IR is far more comfortable with the concept of identity than it is with culture, as evidenced in the slippage of meaning between the two terms and with the bulk of work in this literature which concerns itself with identity-based issues (Reeves, 1998). Rather than abandon existing theory or following what they see as the reductionist path to individualistic security logic, Buzan and Wæver have attempted to devise 'a theoretical conception of identity-related security issues at the unit level, which was therefore interoperable with classical security theory' (1997, p. 242).

The approach developed by this so-called Copenhagen school in a number of works (Weaver *et al.*, 1990; Buzan *et al.*, 1990; Wæver *et al.*, 1993) tries to argue 'how societies defined in terms of identity could be seen as the referent object for some cases of securitisation, where that which could be lost was not sovereignty but identity' (Buzan and Wæver, 1997, p. 242). Key to this new concern in their work about identity has been the way in which things other than the state can become the object of security discourse. This seems an interesting point as Buzan and Wæver claim that constructivism in security studies can show how security issues do not exist in and of themselves but are defined as a result of political processes.

The benefits of this approach are clear for retaining, and not contradicting, the state centrism of classical security studies. By shifting and progressing the referent object of security analysis to societal security they are able to consider the post-Cold War security environment with more analytical tools, albeit still linked to the state. The individual and community level is dealt with in a certain way in this framework – the position therefore remains close to the earlier work of Buzan where the state retains state-level attributes which cannot be reassembled from individual level attributes and where the state needs to retain a unit level reality. Individual security can be studied from this perspective, following the above, because it is implicated in 'all action that fulfils the criteria of being a security speech act' (Buzan and Wæver, 1997, p. 245). From this position, one can understand individuals and their role in social process and society as a whole, while being able to grasp the securitization process (which takes place at the state and international level) to define referent objects of security, whilst also managing larger international formulations such as regional security complexes.

This approach acknowledges its inability to address emancipatory questions about the 'real' security of marginalized groups who do not articulate security demands in any powerful way, and who therefore do not have their security demands heard or considered within the securitization process. However, the lack of concern for the marginal is clear – power and powerful security claims are those which can be voiced, heard and considered within a largely state-based framework. The problem with this approach from the position emphasized in this book is the lack of an account of the void this critical space leaves theoretically, and more importantly, practically, for the marginalized. Critiques of this position (McSweeney, 1996) partly try to address this lack of concern for the marginal through wanting to see the term 'society' treated in theoretical analysis as 'a process of negotiating, affirmation and reproduction [as a] system of inter-relationships which connects together individuals who share a common culture' (pp. 82–3). This position understands society as fluid and constantly reconstructing itself and highlights the relevance of cultural analysis in IR discussions of security.

Culture is often used in IR in conceptually undifferentiated ways and the different contexts in which it could be related to security – to identity in a variety of forms, spaces and places as opposed to territory, or cultural autonomy through practices and process – require a more thorough engagement with cultural theory. It can be said, however, that the shift from security as static in a state-based framework to one where politically normative issues are being discussed suggests there exist different ways of knowing and understanding security in a variety of contexts (see Chan, 1997, and Afterword).

A second set of issues is raised by the book's emphasis on a more societal approach to security analysis. This does not preclude interest in how this level links with other levels of analysis, primarily the state, within complex social systems. The approach emphasized in this book does not abandon the security relationship between the individual and the state within a community approach. Indeed, focus on the community level requires placement within the wider social context lest it falls into the trap of isolation. The study of security within complex social systems does require understanding of the linkages between the state in its different forms, processes and practices which work in and around the level of community. It requires further discussion about community identity, culture and security and how this remains relevant to more traditional security interests such as inter-community violence.

Third, some of the book's key arguments – drawn as they are from the assumption that the third world's structural location in the global political economy, along with other social and political pressures such as environmental degradation and the increasing need to address pressing issues of poverty and inequality both politically and normatively – are forcing IR to broaden its security agenda. This shift from traditional approaches to security to the fractured debate we currently have is symbolic and has implications for the future of security studies.

For instance, the growing pressures of the global environment discussed in Chapter 7 and the linkages between poverty and the environment are an important area of concern. Most significantly, the whole discourse of global environmental problems is being framed in such a way that makes those marginalized in an ecological sense become the threat. Thus it is the planet which has generally been depicted as the referent of security; the lives of the poor only become securitized to the extent that they threaten global security. Thus, at the Rio conference of 1992 (United Nations Conference on Environment and Development; UNCED), there was discussion of women and poverty but not of men and affluence.

The links between poverty, security and development discussed in Chapter 6 emphasize Dalby's (1997) suggestion that the shift to incorporate politically normative interests in security studies is a far more subversive enterprise within IR than its more orthodox predecessor (in Krause and Williams, 1997). The debate witnessed around Booth's call for emancipatory security, as an example, illustrates the need for further empirical and theoretical investigation (see Booth, 1990, 1991a, 1991b). The practicalities of an emancipatory security approach have yet to be grounded within concrete third world contexts, incorporating research methods which, as far as possible, allow for the poor and marginalized to define and voice what their needs are. Here is a clear indication of the benefits which could be gained from an interdisciplinary approach involving critical security studies and Development Studies.

Concluding Remarks

Despite preferences, this book has not sought to use an unnecessarily polemic tone. Whilst we feel it a positive development that IR has gone beyond fixed conceptions of security, and whilst suggesting the value of a micro-security approach, this does not mean that a pragmatic military approach to security is irrelevant in all contexts. For us it is important that students, and indeed scholars, of IR regard it as an enterprise about thinking; IR should not be an unthinking social science. When lack of certainty becomes the only certainty, IR will not become irrelevant, it will have become possible for it to be relevant much more than it is now in a range of contexts beyond those with which it has traditionally been associated. Rethinking security has been, is being and will be a crucial facet of IR.

References

Booth, K. (1990) *New Thinking about Strategy and International Security*. London: Unwin Hyman.
Booth, K. (1991a) 'Security and emancipation', *Review of International Studies*, 17 (3), 313–26.
Booth, K. (1991b) 'Security in anarchy: utopian realism in theory and practice', *International Affairs*, 67 (3), 527–45.
Buzan, B. et al. (1990) *The European Security Agenda Recast: Scenarios for the Post-Cold War Era*. London: Pinter.
Buzan, B. and Wæver, O. (1997) 'Slippery? Contradictory? Sociologically untenable? The Copenhagen school replies', *Review of International Studies*, 23 (2), 241–50.
Buzan, B., Wæver, O. and De Wilde, J. (1997) *Security: New Frameworks for Analysis*. Boulder, CO: Lynne Rienner.
Chan, S. (1997) 'Seven types of ambiguity in Western international relations theory and painful steps towards right ethics', *Theoria: A Journal of Social and Political Theory*, June, 106–15.

Dalby, S. (1997) 'Contesting an essential concept: reading the dilemmas in contemporary security disclosure'. In Krause, K. and Williams, M. (eds) *Critical Security Studies: Concepts and Cases*. London: UCL Press, pp. 3–31.

Der Derian, J. 'The value of security: Hobbes, Marx, Nietzsche and Baudrillard'. In Campbell, D. and Dillon, M. (eds) (1993) *The Political Subject of Violence*. Manchester: Manchester University Press, pp. 94–109.

Krause, J. and Renwick, N. (eds) (1996) *Identities in International Relations*. Basingstoke: Macmillan.

Lapid, Y. and Kratochwil, F. (eds) (1997) *The Return of Culture and Identity in International Relations Theory*. Boulder, CO: Lynne Rienner.

McSweeney, B. (1996) 'Identity and security: Buzan and the Copenhagen school', *Review of International Studies*, 22 (1), 81–93.

Reeves, J. (1998) 'Culture and identity: ships that ought to pass in the night'. CRIPT Spring Term Workshop, Keele University, 7 March.

Wæver, O. et al. (eds) (1990) *European Polyphony: Perspectives beyond East–West Confrontation*. London: Macmillan.

Wæver, O. et al. (1993) *Identity, Migration and the New Security Agenda in Europe*. London: Pinter.

Afterword: Signing the Swamplands

STEPHEN CHAN
*Professor of International Relations and Ethics,
Nottingham Trent University*

The future of International Relations (IR) may be very different from its past. When, in 1918, David Davies endowed the first professorship in the subject at Aberystwyth, named the Woodrow Wilson Chair in support of open diplomacy, he hoped that knowledge and thought could act as a substitute for war (see Porter, 1989). IR has had a very poor track record. The legacy of Davies has not stopped a single war with the strength of its knowledge, and the rhetorical claim that it might yet speak truth to power has floundered upon bitter divisions as to how anything might be proved truthful. The wood has not been seen for the trees, and navigating even the trees has been like taking a walk through the Florida Everglades. The swamplands of the discipline might well lead students to ask, with justified exasperation, whether the trip can be worthwhile.

The debate that followed Davies may be said to have had three stages. I express what these were a little differently from others. The first stage concerned the question as to what acts or thoughts caused states to begin or refrain from war. The second stage showed a subtle shift: *who* acts to cause or prevent wars? The third stage, more subtle still, asked two questions: *why* do people internationalize themselves – as individuals, groups, classes, companies, organizations, or states – for the sake of peace and war? What is the moral content of such internationalization?

The problem here is that whilst the debate has been conducted, it has also left nothing behind. Each layer continues to have its adherents. They do, however, *refine* the layer they champion. What sort of brief sociology can be proposed for these adherents or champions, particularly as they address the matter of security?

First, some seek to add new insights to security to their basic arguments, without sacrificing any of those arguments. The neorealism of Barry Buzan, in its marriage to the Copenhagen school, is a perfect example of this.

Second, some seek to categorize the discipline, either to make it orderly or for the sake of teaching it, as John Groom has tried to do (see Olson and Groom, 1992), or problematize it as Steve Smith has tried to do (see Smith, 1995). Groom, however, barely disguises the fact that, in so doing, he is a champion of pluralist IR, and his other 'paradigms' have strawmen qualities about them.

Third, some seek to reinvent the discipline, especially its moral concern, or rather only its moral context, by marrying IR to other disciplines, particularly moral philosophy. The elegant, if instant syntheses by Chris Brown of condensed and selective German idealism are an epitome here (see Brown, 1992).

Fourth, there is a sliding scale from this last category to the next, and that is the urge to question the discipline to the point of deconstructing it – or even to the point of deconstructing the world itself, or whatever large part of it seemed visibly international. Probably, the sliding scale would involve Campbell (1992), Walker (1992) and Der Derian (1992) in that order, towards the temptation of total deconstruction.

Fifth, alternatively it might be possible, and it is amazing how much a minority this represents, to reinvestigate IR – and security – by asking its basic questions anew. I believe that the authors of this book have achieved a service for students by seeking to do this. In their conclusions they have made a mature and sensible assessment of the state of security studies, couched within an assessment of the state of IR. This is not an inconsiderable achievement.

What, however, remains to be done in the future? After all, a firm footing in the swamp does not lead you out of the swamp. I do not know if we shall get out of the swamp. The world becomes more complex, and thought on the world – even balanced on secure footholds in the world – becomes also more complex. However, IR has fought shy of two enquiries in particular.

The first is that, despite some tentative efforts, the question of cultural difference, particularly in the construction of moral philosophy, is not embedded in IR. There are few champions within mainstream debates, alluded to above, who are also protagonists of *some* cognition of culture and its effect on moral purpose and action in world politics. Piscatori (1986) and Halliday (1996) are distinguished exceptions here.

The second is that there are barely any efforts at all on the question of psychological animation in IR debates and the quest for security. The French psycholinguistic thinkers enter IR only to deconstruct the project of universalism, but not to pose questions of fear, loathing and messy interiority. John Burton made a primitive attempt at the importation of psychological practice, against an equally primitive assessment of psychological needs (see Burton, 1997). On the periphery of IR George Bull's *International Minds* journal, associated with the Coventry University and Coventry Cathedral Centre for Forgiveness and Reconciliation, has hardly entered any deep consistency, even on its own terms. Of Waltz's famous three images, IR has chosen steadfastly the third, the international system, but is there not the possibility, within the universalized world, for difference, right down to the difference of individual fears in the face of individual security?

The book and the Afterword depart. The world remains a place isolated from security. David Davies hoped that thought and knowledge would overcome war and insecurity. It has not yet. Perhaps a future student generation, like an amphibian emerging from a swamp, trying out its legs on dryish ground, will think and know better than we can today. I hope this book will help.

References

Brown, C. (1992) *International Relations Theory: New Normative Approaches*. Hemel Hempstead: Harvester Wheatsheaf.
Burton, J. (1997) *Violence Explained*. Manchester: Manchester University Press.
Campbell, D. (1992) *Writing Security: United States Foreign Policy and the Politics of Identity*. Manchester: Manchester University Press.
Der Derian, J. (1992) *Anti-Diplomacy: Spies, Terror, Speed and War*. Oxford: Blackwell.
Halliday, F. (1996) *Islam and the Myth of Confrontation*. London: I.B. Tauris.
Olson, W. and Groom, A.J.R. (1992) *International Relations: Then and Now*. London: Routledge.
Piscatori, J.P. (1986) *Islam in a World of Nation-States*. Cambridge: Cambridge University Press.
Porter, B. (1989) 'David Davies: a hunter after peace', *Review of International Studies*, 15 (1), 27–36.
Smith, S. (1995) 'The self-images of a discipline: a genealogy of international relations theory'. In Booth, K. and Smith, S. (eds) *International Relations Theory Today*. Cambridge: Polity Press, pp. 1–37.
Walker, R.B.J. (1992) *Inside/Outside: International Relations as Political Theory*. Cambridge: Cambridge University Press.

Index

Adams, W. 132
Adorno, T. 61
Afghanistan 26
Africa 2, 25, 28, 50, 85
  see also under individual companies
agency 45, 47, 111–12, 119, 126
Ali, S. 25
anarchism 83, 88
anarchy 43–4, 62, 112, 117
anthropocentrism 77, 85–6
anti-modernism 136
arms races 44, 96
Ashley, Richard 47
Asia 25, 28, 50
  East 30
  Southeast 30, 45
  see also under individual countries
atomic bomb 96
atomism 11
Ayoob, M. 5, 13, 27, 50–3, 131

'backward discipline' 4, 29, 57
Bacon Francis 76–7
Bahro, R. 74, 79, 87–8, 137, 144
balance of power 6, 41, 43–4, 82, 117
Banks, M. 8–9
Bauldrillard, J. 68
Beck, Ulrich 3, 53
Bhopal 79
biocentrism 89

see also ecocentrism
Bolivia 37, 132–3, 137–44
Bookchin, M. 87
Booth, K. 8, 10, 12–14, 48, 63, 69, 114, 125
Brazil 32
Brundtland Commission 80, 137–44
Burton, J. 131
Buzan, B. 4, 9–14, 45, 48–54, 57–8, 63, 73, 94, 131

Clavert, P. 8
Campaign for Nuclear Disarmament (CND) 96
Campbell, D. 3, 60, 70, 82, 84, 89
capital, international 111
capitalism 63, 113, 121, 137
Carr, E. H. 43, 63
Carson, R. 79
Central America 85
  see also under individual countries
Chad 15, 22, 32
Chan, S. 32
Chernobyl (Ukraine) 79
China 32, 34
  see also revolution, Chinese
Chomsky, N. 7
civil society 112, 140
  global 112, 136
civilization 22-3, 77

Index

Cold War 2, 11–12, 16, 24, 26, 31, 41, 43, 74, 80, 93, 100–1, 115, 117
collective security 5
communism 29, 31
community 23, 37, 51, 74, 78, 104, 117, 119
  security 105, 122
comprehensive security 4
conservation 83
conservatism 5, 13, 83, 85, 94, 100
Copenhagen School 115
coping strategies 52, 109, 121
Cox, Robert 61
critical theory, *see under* theory
critique 52–3, 58, 65, 88, 98, 113, 148
  Marxist 97
Crush, J. 30
Cuban Missile Crisis 97
culture 17, 78, 88, 115, 120–1, 151

Dalby, S. 113, 115–16, 119, 153
debt 139
democracy 30, 50, 65, 74, 142
  participatory 87, 142
Der Derian, J. 67–8, 148
Descartes, René 76–7
determinism 65, 68
Deudney, D. 4, 11, 47, 74, 82, 84
Deutsch, K. 97
development 17, 26, 33–4, 50, 67, 78, 80, 85
  studies, *see* Development Studies
  sustainable 17, 73, 78, 80, 85, 93, 106, 131–44
Development Studies 1, 30, 108–27, 154
Devetak, R. 61–2
diplomacy, environmental 81, 83
discourse 22, 33, 37 n.1, 53, 62, 64–6, 69, 105, 111, 117–18, 124, 136, 142
  universalizing 132, 138
Dobson, A. 74, 86–8, 134
Dunn, D. 98, 102

Easter Island 79
Eckersley, R. 77, 86
ecocentrism 77
  see also biocentrism
ecological philosophies 17, 73–89
  eco-audit 135
  eco-fascism 86
  eco-feminism 69, 78
  eco-imperialism 78
  eco-labelling 135
  eco-socialism 75
ecological shadow 88, 139
ecology 11, 33, 51
  deep 75, 77
elites 15, 50, 141
emancipation 13–14, 35, 63, 84, 114–15, 125, 143
Enlightenment 30, 63–4, 76, 87, 110
Enloe, C. 114
environmental degradation 10, 34, 78, 80, 85, 114, 118, 134, 153
  see also under threat
environmental issues 15, 17, 73–89
environmentalism 73–89
  shallow 75
epistemic communities 10, 83
epistemology 4, 12, 14, 18, 23, 53, 57, 59, 65, 68, 98, 100, 105, 115, 117, 150
Escobar, A. 29, 36, 67, 123, 140
ethics 4, 14, 53, 57, 115
ethnography 119
etymology 23

Falk, R. 5, 13, 73
Falkland Islands 98
favelas 35

feminism 16, 59, 60, 68–70, 102, 149
  conservative 69
  liberal 69
  Marxist 69
  psychoanalytical 69
  radical 69
  see also eco-feminism
first world 24, 34, 108
food security 108–9, 147–8
forests 86
Foucault, M. 65, 67
Frankfurt School 61
Fukuyama, F. 30, 143

Galeano, E. 101
Galtung, J. 6, 13, 73–4, 94, 97
gender 69–70, 86, 99–100, 102–3
  see also feminism
genealogy 60, 67
genocide 100
geography 16, 81
  political 103, 150
George, J. 4, 46, 53, 57–8, 60, 66–7
Giddens, A. 53
global political economy, *see* political economy
global security 14
globalization 14–15, 34, 37, 78, 106, 111, 113, 119, 121, 148
God 25, 76
Gramsci, A. 62–3, 137
grassroots organizations (GROs) 8, 125, 135
Greece 29
greens, German 137
gross national product (GNP) 32, 34
Group of 77 26
growth 34, 87–8, 131, 134, 140, 143
Guatemala 29
Gulf States 2

Habermas, J. 61
Haiti 16
Hannerz, U. 120–2
Hayward, Tim 77–8, 89, 141
health 103, 108
  security 147
Hitler, Adolf 46
Hobbes, Thomas 69
Hoffman, Mark 61
holism 11, 36
Honduras 16
Horkheimer, M. 61
Hovden, E. 76, 80
human
  nature 47
  needs 34
  rights 15, 100–1
  security 4, 115, 142–4
Hungary 96

ideal type 35
idealism 5, 43, 83
identity 17, 43, 120–1, 151
ideology 25, 65
  see also individual ideologies
'impact on' approach 69
imperialism 25, 29, 123
  see also eco-imperialism
India 22, 32, 79
indigenous peoples 51, 85
individualism 64, 88
Indonesia 32
industrial society, *see under* society
inequality 83
injustice 5, 24, 136
insecurity 14, 44, 48, 50, 62, 88, 101, 104
  spiral of 44
  see also security
interdependence 8–9, 45
international political economy, *see* political economy

International Union for the Conservation of Nature (IUCN) 80
inter-paradigm debate 8–9, 75
intertextual relations 65
Italy 22

Japan 22
Jervis, R. 44
Journal of Conflict Resolution 95–6, 99
Journal of Peace Research 95, 97

Kant, Immanuel 30, 61
Keohane, R. 9
Khrushchev, Nikita 97
King, Martin Luther 97
knowledge 65, 68, 85, 120, 133
Koffman, S. 6
Kothari, R. 30, 113

Laos 32, 37, 105
Latin America 25–6, 28, 50, 136, 141
law 99
Lawler, P. 93, 98–100
least developed countries (LLDCs) 32
left, the 29, 83
Lesotho 120
less developed countries (LDCs) 32
liberalism 30, 43, 75, 124, 135, 137
lifestyles 78, 86, 88–9, 144
Limits to Growth report 80
Linklater, A. 46, 61–2, 87
Lippman, W. 6
Lopez, G. 99
Lukes, S. 10

Machiavelli, Niccolò 67, 69
Marcuse, Herbert 61
marginalization 24–5, 36, 89, 104, 109, 126
market, the 106, 111, 122, 134, 144
Marshall Plan 29

Marx, Karl 61, 68, 83
Marxism 9, 36, 42, 75
masculinity 69, 102
methodology 12, 36, 57, 65, 95, 100, 116–17, 119, 122, 154
see also individual methodologies
micro-level security 17, 53, 109, 118–24, 126
Middle East 104
migration 103, 115, 147
militarization 7
military 7, 10, 12, 139
see also under threat
modernism 58, 136
modernity 3, 22, 64, 106, 123
Morgenthau, H. 42, 43, 81
Mozambique 16, 29
multinational corporations (MNCs) 8
myths 36, 69, 79, 135

Naess, Arne 74
Naipaul, S. 22, 31
national security 82, 84, 102, 115
natural resources 81
see also resources
nature 74, 77, 84
neoliberalism 37, 83, 111–12, 133, 140, 142
neorealism 41–56, 116–17, 149
Nepal 120
new international economic order (NIEO) 26
new social movements (NSMs) 8
newly industrialized countries (NICs) 2, 32
Nicaragua 22, 29, 32
Nietzche, Friedrich Wilhelm 68
nihilism 66
nimbyism 78
Nkrumah, Kwame 31
Non-Aligned Movement (NAM) 24, 26

non-governmental organizations (NGOs)   8, 10, 83, 104, 109, 112, 120, 124–6, 139
normative approaches   17, 53, 61, 98, 109, 127, 147–8, 153
North–South issues   16, 84, 86
nuclear accidents   104
nuclear proliferation   15

ontology   9, 12–13, 53, 57, 62, 67, 105
oppression   36, 69, 86
orthodoxy   13, 16, 30, 41, 63, 76, 93, 100, 104, 111, 136
over-consumption   10, 15, 75, 114, 136
ozone   104

pacifism   95, 98
peace   4, 95, 97, 100
Peace Research Institute Oslo (PRIO)   95
Peace Studies   6, 13, 73, 93–102, 150
peasants   85, 123, 139
philosophy   62, 64, 67, 74, 76, 80, 84, 94, 104, 134, 148
pluralism   8–9, 83
political economy   25–6, 86, 94, 104, 112–13, 115, 153
pollution   79, 118
popular participation   139, 141–2
population   87, 147
Porritt, J.   88
Portugal   15, 33
positivism   47, 52, 65
postmodernism   57–8, 64–8, 104
poststructuralism   47, 57, 59, 104
poverty   5, 24, 29–30, 34, 63, 69, 75, 88, 109, 113, 115–16, 118, 124, 140, 153
  absolute   28
  relative   33
  structural   15

power   10, 43, 61, 65, 67, 81, 113, 143
Prebisch, R.   26
psychology   16, 24, 31, 99

race   69–70
radicalism   49, 75, 86, 97, 134
rationality   77, 113
re-cycling   89
realism   5, 8–10, 14, 18, 25, 34, 41–56, 58, 65–6, 69, 82, 103, 105
reformism   86
resistance   52, 74
resources   44, 98, 118, 139–40
  see also natural resources
revolution
  behavioural   80
  Chinese   30
  French   24
  industrial   79
  scientific   76
Richardson, L.F.   96
Rio Conference, *see* United Nations Conference on Environment and Development
Rio + 5   80
risk   3, 79
Rist, G.   33
Romania   29
Rostow, W.   33, 50

Saad, S.   15
Sanchez de Lozada, G.   140
Saurin, J.   3, 111, 127
Schmid, H.   97
second world   15, 31, 34
security
  complexes   45
  referent of   9–11, 22, 27, 48, 115, 152
  theoretical development of   2–15
  see also individual types
Security Dialogue   95

Seers, D.   34
Shaw, M.   48–9, 53, 57, 93
Shiva, V.   76
Simpsons, The   33
Sklair, L.   78, 133
socialism   63, 83, 88
  see also eco-socialism
societal security   117–18, 152
society   51, 86
  industrial   74, 87, 135
sociology   9, 48, 53, 68, 93–4, 102, 150
  historical   94
South Korea   15–16, 29, 33
Spykman, N.   81
states   32, 63, 110, 112
  important   45
  sovereign   5, 8, 64, 116
  weak   45, 50–1
Stockholm Conference, *see* United Nations Conference on the Human Environment
Strategic Studies   5–7, 12, 16, 41, 80, 105
structuralism   8–9, 23, 25–6, 47
Sweden   95, 97
Syvester, Christine   114

Taiwan   142
theoretical tools   2, 21, 75, 105, 116, 150
theory   13, 59, 66–7
  critical   16, 58, 61–3, 83, 103, 149
  dependency   26–8
  mainstream   42, 83
  modernization   18, 23, 27–8, 33, 104
  political   78
  problem-solving   62, 78, 82–3
  social   57, 95
  see aso individual theories
third world
  debt   10, 101

economics   10
  see also individual countries
threat   11, 46, 50, 62, 70
  environmental   82
  military   82
Three Mile Island   79
Thucydides   43, 67
Tickner, J.A.   4, 43, 69, 102, 114
transnational corporations, *see* multinational corporations
truth   64–8, 88, 133, 143

United Nations Conference on Environment and Development (UNCED)   138–9, 153
United Nations Conference on the Human Environment (UNCHE)   80
United Nations Development Programme (UNDP)   108
United States   22, 30, 35, 79, 96, 110, 117
utopias   14, 76, 83, 88, 137

Vasquez, J.   44
Vietnam   26, 105
violence   97, 116, 153
  structural   98–9, 101
Vogler, J.   88

Wallerstein, I.   25
Walt, S.   4, 11, 37, 46, 58, 67
Waltz, K.   42–3, 81
war   6, 12, 44, 46, 94, 99, 117
  see also Cold War
water   81
  security   104
Westphalia   5, 50–1
Wilde, Oscar   14
Wolfers, A.   5, 42
World Order Models Project (WOMP)   73
Wright, Q.   96

zero-sum logic   14, 44